C000151564

eat in

the best food is made at home

for mum and dad

thanks for your generous love and support, and for letting me make
a huge mess in the kitchen when I was little ... and big!

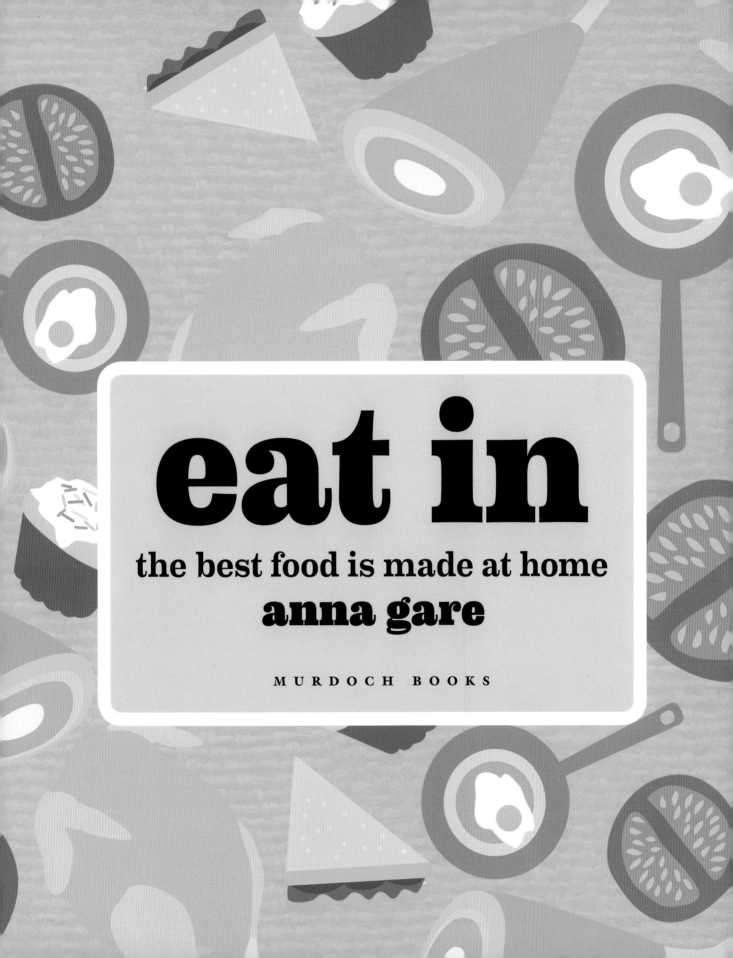

eat in

the best food is made at home
anna gare

MURDOCH BOOKS

contents

introduction

I am a shameless food lover. It seems that every great moment in my life has involved food — or is it that the moments just seem greater when there is food involved?

I was once asked to describe the best meal of my life. As I ploughed through all of the fabulous meals I have eaten, the ones that burst out of my cloudy memory with the most clarity were the simple ones involving family, friends, holidays and special occasions.

I'll never forget the day I pan-fried a coral trout with a lemon lime beurre blanc and served it with crispy iceberg lettuce. I had spent all day in a dinghy at the Montebello Islands, in and out of the water, chasing fish with hooks and stinky old bait with no luck. And then, as the day ran out of puff, one very generous and fat coral trout decided to grace my hook — hence our dinner table.

I had eaten coral trout before, but this fish tasted of the whole day. I had earned this beautiful morsel and every bite told the story: the crispiness of the sun, the saltiness of the ocean and the sweet floral flavour only a coral trout has. My palette was harmonising with the feel of the place.

I love to eat, but most of all I love to cook and I always have. I love the whole process of preparation and feeding people. I don't find cooking a chore. For me, it's a creative outlet and a pleasure that everyone benefits from.

This book is about making simple yummy food with fresh ingredients. I really believe you don't have to spend hours in the kitchen to make spectacular food. I get more excited when I cook something delicious with little effort, than I do when I make something fiddly and complicated.

Cooking, like love, does not have to be rocket science. It is a way of thinking, tasting and feeling that allows you to draw pleasure out of what could otherwise be ordinary. It turns a chore into a little party, or, sometimes, a big one.

The best food is made at home, so *Eat In* and use some of my favourite recipes to indulge your cravings and treat the people you love.

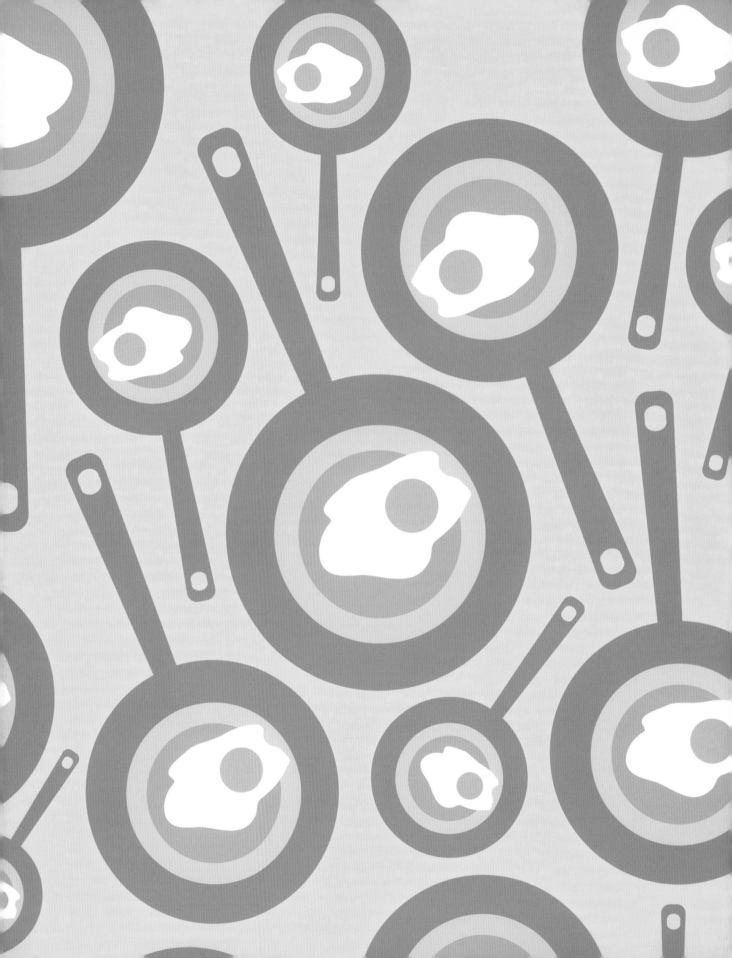

good morning

I'm a morning girl. I love getting up early, turning on the tunes and waking up the kids. They are teenagers now so they like to sleep in, and I have to admit that I take just a dash of perverse pleasure in getting them up. It's pay-back time!

During the week we usually help ourselves to cereal and fruit, or a simple poached egg on toast. But when the weekend comes we love to cook, and breakfast the necessity suddenly becomes breakfast the joy.

A cooked breakfast often speaks of having had a big night or of laying the foundations for a big day ahead. Either way, it celebrates escaping from the mundane cereal world into an orchestra of flavours and aromas that wake up our senses.

It's a meal we don't always plan for. It's driven by our mood, our taste buds and whatever is handy in the fridge. The smell of the weekend fry-up — coffee brewing, eggs sizzling, bread toasting — lures the kids out from under their blankets. There's nothing like a cruisey morning without the crush of the daily agenda.

There are as many ways of making breakfast a pleasure as there are days in the year. In this chapter I'm sharing a few of my favourites with you.

spiced fruit compote

Fills a 1 litre (35 fl oz/4 cup) capacity jar

This is a fantastic fruit compote made from dried fruits spiced up with a splash of rum, some cloves and cinnamon. It keeps in the fridge for a few months and is a great alternative to fresh fruit.

INGREDIENTS

300 g (10½ oz/1½ cups) pitted
   prunes (see Note)
185 g (6½ oz/1 cup) dried figs
180 g (6¼ oz/1 cup) dried pears
155 g (5½ oz/1 cup) dried apricots
50 g (1¾ oz/½ cup) dried apples
110 g (3¾ oz/½ cup) caster
   (superfine) sugar
750 ml (26 fl oz/3 cups) freshly
   squeezed orange juice
625 ml (21½ fl oz/2½ cups) water
60 ml (2 fl oz/¼ cup) dark rum
   (optional)
4 whole cloves
1 cinnamon stick

METHOD

Put all of the ingredients into a large saucepan and bring to the boil over medium heat.

Reduce the heat to low and simmer for 10 minutes.

Remove from the heat and allow to cool in the pan.

Spoon the cooled compote into a 1 litre (35 fl oz/4 cup) capacity jar, seal and refrigerate.

Keeps really well in the fridge and improves with age.

Enjoy it immediately with porridge, on muesli (granola) or simply served with yoghurt at any time of the day.

NOTE When measuring out the dried fruits, make sure they are firmly packed cups.

nasi goreng

Serves 4

Lazy holidays in Bali introduced me to nasi goreng for breakfast. There are many variations of this dish, which can be served at any time of the day. It's very popular as a breakfast and great to make when you have leftover rice. I always keep some fresh turmeric and galangal in my freezer so I can whip this up whenever I have the urge for something really flavoursome.

METHOD

Heat the peanut oil in a wok over high heat. Add the shallots, turmeric, ginger, garlic, galangal, most of the chilli, lemongrass, dried shrimp, lime leaves (if using) and star anise, and stir-fry for a few minutes to soften.

Add the bacon and green beans and stir-fry for a few more minutes to lightly cook the bacon.

Toss in the cooked rice, kecap manis and tomato sauce, and stir to heat the rice through.

Add the spinach just before serving and taste for seasoning.

Top with a poached or crispy fried egg, scatter over the crispy shallots and serve with the extra chilli and kecap manis at the table.

NOTES You can buy fresh turmeric and galangal in Asian grocers. I buy more than I need and keep it in the freezer, but you can use ground turmeric for this if need be.

I like to use basmati rice. To get 4 cups of cooked rice, you will need 265 g (9¼ oz/1⅓ cups) of uncooked rice.

Kecap manis is an Indonesian sweet soy sauce sold in good Asian grocers. It can be substituted with soy sauce sweetened with a little brown sugar.

Crispy shallots are available from the Asian section of most supermarkets, or Asian grocers.

INGREDIENTS

60 ml (2 fl oz/¼ cup) peanut oil

4 red Asian shallots, thinly sliced

2 teaspoons finely grated fresh turmeric (see Notes)

2 teaspoons finely grated fresh ginger

3 garlic cloves, minced

2 teaspoons finely grated fresh galangal (see Notes)

1 large red chilli, thinly sliced

1 lemongrass stem, pale part only, finely chopped

1 teaspoon dried ground shrimp

2 kaffir lime leaves, thinly sliced (optional)

pinch of ground star anise

180 g (6¼ oz) bacon, thinly sliced

100 g (3½ oz) green beans, trimmed and chopped into 1 cm (½ inch) pieces

740 g (1 lb 10 oz/4 cups) cooked rice (see Notes)

1 tablespoon kecap manis, plus extra to serve (see Notes)

squirt of tomato sauce (ketchup)

handful of baby spinach

4 poached or crispy fried eggs

crispy shallots, to serve (see Notes)

huevos rancheros

Serves 4

This is a Mexican-inspired breakfast, and it makes for a delicious weekend brunch. I often make it when I have leftover bean mix from tacos the night before. I'm big on chilli in the morning and I've finally converted the kids, too. You can spice this recipe up as much as you like.

INGREDIENTS

4 tortillas (18 cm/7 inches in diameter)
100 g (3½ oz) thinly shaved Manchego cheese
4 eggs
sour cream, to serve
chilli sauce, to serve (optional)

BEAN MIX

2 tablespoons olive oil
½ red onion, finely diced
80 g (2¾ oz) thinly sliced smoky pancetta (optional)
1 habanero chilli, seeded and thinly sliced
2 garlic cloves, minced
1 heaped teaspoon smoked sweet paprika
4 big ripe tomatoes, finely chopped
125 ml (4 fl oz/½ cup) water
sea salt and freshly ground black pepper
1 x 400 g (14 oz) tin four-bean mix, drained and rinsed

RED SALSA

2 roma (plum) tomatoes, seeded and finely diced
¼ small red onion, finely diced
squeeze of lime juice
drizzle of extra virgin olive oil
pinch of caster (superfine) sugar
pinch of sea salt and freshly ground black pepper

GREEN SALSA

1 small avocado, stone removed, finely diced
2 tablespoons coriander (cilantro) leaves, finely chopped
1 jalapeňo chilli, finely diced
squeeze of lime juice
drizzle of extra virgin olive oil
pinch of caster (superfine) sugar
pinch of sea salt

METHOD

Preheat the oven to 180°C (350°F/Gas 4).

TO MAKE THE BEAN MIX

Heat the olive oil in a heavy-based frying pan over low–medium heat then add the onion, pancetta (if using), chilli, garlic and paprika, and cook for a few minutes, or until the onions have softened.

Add the tomato and water, season with salt and pepper and simmer for 10 minutes.

Add the beans and simmer for 10 minutes, stirring occasionally so the mix doesn't stick to the base of the pan.

TO MAKE THE RED SALSA

Combine all of the ingredients and set aside.

TO MAKE THE GREEN SALSA

Combine all of the ingredients and set aside.

TO MAKE THE HUEVOS RANCHEROS

Put the tortillas on a baking tray and top each one with cheese and then the bean mix (leave a little well in the middle for the egg).

Bake for 5 minutes, then remove from the oven.

Crack an egg into the middle of each tortilla and return to the oven for 10 minutes, or until the eggs are cooked to your liking.

Top the tortillas with a spoonful of each salsa and serve with a nice dollop of sour cream. I always add some chilli sauce because I like it hot!

turkish bullseye

Serves 6

Sometimes timing the eggs and the toast while trying to juggle kid chaos and a whistling kettle in the mornings can be too much. That's why 'bullseye' is an easy favourite in our house: the eggs and the bread cook together at the same time, and there's only one dirty dish to wash. You can make this with any kind of bread, but my favourite bread in the world is Turkish flat bread — especially when it's fresh from the bakery. The beauty of this dish is that you can cook up to six at a time in a big roasting tray on the stovetop, and also eat it on the run.

INGREDIENTS

softened butter, for spreading
    and cooking
1 long Turkish flat bread (pide)
    about 2–3 cm ($\frac{3}{4}$–1$\frac{1}{4}$ inches) thick
6 eggs

METHOD

Lightly butter both sides of the bread, then cut into six rectangles, about 12 x 10 cm (4$\frac{1}{2}$ x 4 inches).

Use a 5–6 cm (2–2$\frac{1}{2}$ inch) round cookie cutter to cut out the centre from each rectangle of bread.

Place a large flameproof roasting tray over high heat. When hot, arrange the bread in the tray.

Put a little dob of butter into each hole, then crack an egg into each one.

Cook for about 2 minutes on one side, then carefully, but quickly, turn over and cook for another 2 minutes, or until the eggs are cooked to your liking.

Serve right away, with your favourite toppings. I love this with luscious toppings such as crispy bacon and avocado salsa, crumbled feta and a sprinkle of dukkah, or a spoonful of nice relish.

dad's cumquat marmalade

Fills 6 x 200 ml (7 fl oz) capacity jars

My dad makes the best marmalade I have ever tasted. He plants the tree, picks the fruit, stirs the pot and brings it to the breakfast table, where we all reap the rewards of his harvest ... This is his method. His basic quantities of fruit to water and sugar are foolproof, and guarantee a delicious marmalade every time. If you store it (unopened) in a cool, dry place it will last for years. Once open, store in the fridge and use within the month.

INGREDIENTS

1.5 kg (3 lb 5 oz) cumquats
700 ml (24 fl oz) water, or as needed
660 g (1 lb 7 oz/3 cups) caster
    (superfine) sugar, or as needed
250 ml (9 fl oz/1 cup) freshly
    squeezed lemon juice, or
    as needed

METHOD

Wash the fruit and remove any stems or leaves.
Halve the fruit at the equator then remove the seeds and put them in a piece of muslin (cheesecloth) and tie with kitchen string.
Put the fruit and bag of seeds into a heavy-based saucepan with enough water to fill the pan just below the level of the fruit.
Cover with a heavy plate to weigh down the fruit in the pan. Leave at room temperature for 24 hours.
The next day, bring the soaked fruit slowly to the boil then gently simmer, stirring occasionally, for 1½ hours, or until reduced by about one-third.
Remove from the heat, cover and leave at room temperature for another 24 hours.
The next day, remove and discard the bag of seeds. Measure the quantity of cooked fruit in cups and return it to the pan.
Add three-quarters of the amount in sugar and one-quarter of the amount in lemon juice to the cooked fruit. For example, if you have 4 cups of cooked fruit, add 3 cups of sugar and 1 cup of lemon juice.
Put the pan over medium heat and boil rapidly for 30 minutes, stirring often to prevent burning. The marmalade is ready when you spoon a bit out onto a cold plate and it sets.
While still hot, transfer the marmalade into warm sterilised jars, seal and store in a cool dry place.
Enjoy on toast with a generous dollop of plain yoghurt.

blueberry smoothie

Serves 2

There's something quite invigorating about a bright purple breakfast!
This smoothie is full of all the good stuff and a great way to sneak a bit of bran
into the kids' diet.

METHOD

Blitz all of the ingredients together in a blender until smooth.

Serve in tall glasses.

NOTES You can use any variety of frozen berries you like for this recipe.

I often peel and freeze my bananas when they start to go brown and use them in smoothies.

INGREDIENTS

150 g (5½ oz/1 cup) frozen blueberries (see Notes)

1 firm, ripe banana (see Notes)

200 g (7 oz/¾ cup) plain yoghurt

juice of 1 orange

1 heaped tablespoon bran

1 teaspoon honey (optional)

poached eggs, spinach, prosciutto & parmesan

Serves 4

Bring back good old-fashioned egg rings! They're a fuss-free way to make perfect poached eggs without the need for vinegar, which I think spoils the flavour. I love this breakfast because of the great combination of flavours and textures: soft poached egg, crisp and salty prosciutto, creamy spinach and tangy tomatoes with a sharp parmesan finish.

METHOD

To make the poached eggs, fill a large, wide frying pan with water, add the salt and bring to the boil over medium heat.

Arrange eight egg rings in the pan and crack an egg into each ring. Reduce the heat to low and poach the eggs until cooked to your liking.

Use an egg slice to remove the eggs and rings, drain on a clean tea towel and put onto a large plate until ready to serve.

Melt the butter in a medium saucepan over medium heat. Add the garlic and cook for about 1 minute, or until softened but not browned.

Add the spinach, cover with a lid and cook for 1–2 minutes, or until wilted.

Heat the olive oil in a separate frying pan over medium heat. When hot, add the prosciutto and cook for a few minutes until crispy, adding the tomatoes at the last minute to warm through.

Pop the toast onto serving plates, top with the spinach, eggs and the prosciutto mixture, scatter over some shaved parmesan and serve immediately.

INGREDIENTS

pinch of salt

8 eggs

20 g (¾ oz) butter

1 garlic clove, minced

180 g (about 6½ oz/1 bunch) English spinach, leaves stripped and washed

drizzle of olive oil

60 g (2¼ oz) thinly sliced prosciutto

105 g (3½ oz/½ cup) semi-dried (sun-blushed) tomatoes

4 thick slices sourdough bread, toasted

shaved parmesan cheese, to garnish

smoked trout omelette

Serves 2

Great for breakfast, lunch or dinner, omelettes are a brilliant way to create a satisfying meal with whatever ingredients you have on hand. Have everything prepared and ready to go (or *'mise en place'* as the professionals say) before you start to cook the omelette.

INGREDIENTS

5 eggs

1 tablespoon milk

sea salt and freshly ground black pepper

20 g (¾ oz) butter

180 g (6¼ oz) smoked rainbow trout (about 1 fillet), skin and bones removed, flaked

2 tablespoons finely sliced red onion

1 tablespoon chopped chives

1 tablespoon coarsely chopped dill

1 teaspoon tiny capers, rinsed

1 heaped tablespoon crème fraîche

METHOD

Lightly whisk the eggs and milk together with a fork and season with salt and pepper. Set aside.

Melt half of the butter in a 15–20 cm (6–8 inch) frying pan over medium heat and tilt the pan to spread it evenly over the base.

Add half of the egg mixture and tilt the pan to spread the egg out evenly. Use a fork to quickly draw the cooked egg from the edge into the centre, tilting the pan to allow any uncooked egg in the middle to run to the edge. Do this about three or four times, until the egg is starting to set. Cook for another 30–40 seconds without stirring, or until the omelette is just set.

Scatter half of the trout, onion, chives, dill and capers over the omelette and spoon over half of the crème fraîche. Gently fold the omelette over in the pan and slide onto a serving plate.

Repeat with the remaining ingredients to make another omelette.

quinoa brekkie

Serves 4

I'm having a bit of an affair with quinoa at the moment and love to wake up to it in the morning. This simple recipe is my take on bircher-style muesli.

METHOD

Wash and strain the quinoa before use, then put into a medium saucepan with the water.

Bring to the boil over medium–high heat.

Reduce the heat to low and simmer, uncovered, for 10 minutes, then add the sultanas and cinnamon, cover with a lid and simmer for 5 minutes. Turn off the heat and allow to cool.

Fold the yoghurt, apple and honey through the cooled quinoa.

Serve in bowls, topped with an extra dollop of yoghurt, the berries and pistachios (if using) and drizzle over some more honey if you have a sweet tooth.

INGREDIENTS

200 g (7 oz/1 cup) white quinoa

500 ml (17 fl oz/2 cups) water

85 g (3 oz/½ cup) sultanas (golden raisins)

pinch of ground cinnamon

200 g (7 oz/¾ cup) plain yoghurt, plus extra to serve

2 apples, grated

1 heaped tablespoon honey, plus extra for drizzling

fresh berries, to serve (optional)

2 tablespoons pistachio nut kernels, to serve (optional)

peach, banana & coconut muffins

Makes 20

There's nothing like a hot muffin straight out of the oven, and these little beauties are buttery, moist and wonderfully dense — just the way I think a muffin should be! The banana gives them a much heavier consistency than those cupcake-like muffins you often find in shops. And, because of that, these keep brilliantly for a couple of days and are perfect when you need to grab something quick on your way out the door in the morning.

INGREDIENTS

350 g (12 oz) unsalted butter, plus extra for greasing

450 g (1 lb/3 cups) self-raising flour, plus extra for dusting (see Note)

110 g (3¾ oz/½ cup, firmly packed) dark brown sugar

110 g (3¾ oz/½ cup) raw sugar

½ teaspoon vanilla bean paste

125 ml (4 fl oz/½ cup) milk

3 eggs

4 ripe bananas, finely chopped (about 1¾ cups)

35 g (1¼ oz/½ cup) shredded coconut

1 teaspoon ground cinnamon

1 x 875 g (1 lb 15 oz) tin sliced peaches, drained

icing (confectioners') sugar, for dusting

METHOD

Preheat the oven to 180°C (350°F/Gas 4).

Lightly grease two 12-hole (80 ml/2½ fl oz/⅓ cup capacity) muffin tins with butter and dust with flour (you'll only need to prepare 20 of the muffin holes).

Melt the butter with the two different sugars in a large saucepan over low heat. Remove from the heat and add the vanilla bean paste and milk. Allow the mixture to cool for a few minutes.

Whisk the eggs into the slightly cooled mixture.

Add the banana, coconut, flour and cinnamon, and stir until well combined.

Count out 20 peach slices and set aside to garnish the tops. Dice the rest of the peach slices and stir into the muffin mixture.

Spoon the mixture into the prepared muffin holes, almost to the top, and decorate each with a reserved peach slice.

Bake for 25 minutes, or until golden, then test with a cake skewer. If it comes out clean, they're ready.

Serve warm or cooled, dusted with icing sugar.

NOTE I've been experimenting with different flours lately and I find that organic and wholemeal ones give these a wonderful earthy flavour. There are big differences in taste between good certified organic flour and regular flour, so I encourage you to experiment and taste the difference for yourself.

cinnamon toast

Serves 1

Once a year, on Mother's Day, the kids bring me breakfast in bed. It's delicious and different every time, but it's always served with love, a handmade card and accompanied by a fresh flower plucked from our garden (or the neighbour's!). I wouldn't swap it for anything in the world. Any other day I think that breakfast in bed is a bit like a picnic on the beach: sounds luxurious, but if you don't do it right you'll end up with crumbs in your bed or sand in your food. I think cinnamon toast is the ideal brekkie in bed because you can eat it with your hands.

METHOD

Whisk the egg, milk and nutmeg (if using) together in a wide, shallow bowl with a fork until well combined.

Dip each slice of bread into the egg mixture and turn it over to coat both sides, allowing the bread to thoroughly soak up the egg mixture.

Sprinkle the sugar and cinnamon onto a plate and mix to distribute evenly. Set aside.

Melt the butter in a non-stick frying pan over low heat and cook the bread for about 2 minutes on each side, or until golden brown. Remove from the pan and immediately coat each side with the sugar mixture.

Enjoy as is, or drizzle with maple syrup if you're feeling decadent.

INGREDIENTS

1 egg

60 ml (2 fl oz/¼ cup) milk

pinch of freshly grated nutmeg (optional)

2 thick slices white bread

1 heaped tablespoon caster (superfine) sugar

½ teaspoon ground cinnamon

10 g (¼ oz) butter

maple syrup, to serve (optional)

lovely lunches

Lunch is the naughty meal; she steals from the morning, borrows from dinner and can hijack a whole day. I think that's why I love her: naughty is just plain fun. Lunch gets bypassed too often, I guess because it's in the middle of our working day. But a big lunch can even turn into a whole week's indulgence in one languid afternoon. Give me a lazy and delectable lunch with friends and I will show you all my teeth.

If I were queen for a day, I would endear myself to my subjects by renaming Wednesday 'Lunchday'. On this day, my subjects would be obliged — in the name of their queen — to round up their loved ones and dear old funny ones alike and spoil them with food love. Lunchday would be a weekly, food-driven, public holiday. We would be in a land of long tables and laughter. My subjects would find joy in the growing, preparation and consumption, but especially in the sharing of their lovely lunch ideas. They would also feel just nicely naughty. This is how it should be. Vote me for queen!

tomato pesto soup

Serves 4–6

If you grow tomatoes and basil together, it will increase the vigour and flavour of both crops; cooking them together produces a similar result.

INGREDIENTS

12–15 ripe tomatoes
2 tablespoons olive oil
2 large brown onions, finely chopped
8 garlic cloves, finely chopped
1 small red chilli, finely chopped (optional)
1 teaspoon sea salt
freshly ground black pepper
750 ml (26 fl oz/3 cups) boiling water
2 x 400 g (14 oz) tins of chopped tomatoes
200 g (7 oz) sour cream, plus extra to serve
250 g (9 oz/1 cup) pesto (see page 155)
small handful of oregano leaves, to serve
4–6 slices of sourdough bread, toasted, to serve

METHOD

Make a criss-cross slit at the top of each tomato and remove the core.

Blanch the tomatoes in boiling water for 1 minute, then refresh under cold water. Peel and discard the skins. Roughly chop the flesh.

Heat the olive oil in a large saucepan over low heat. Add the onion and garlic and cook for 10 minutes, or until the onion is translucent.

Add the fresh tomato, chilli (if using), salt and a pinch or two of pepper. Simmer for 10 minutes, or until the tomato has softened.

Pour in the boiling water and tinned tomatoes and simmer for 30 minutes, or until the soup has thickened nicely and slightly reduced.

Allow the soup to cool slightly, then carefully pour into a blender with the sour cream and pesto (reserve a little pesto for serving). Blend until nice and smooth.

Return the soup to the pan to reheat then divide between the serving bowls and top each with a little extra sour cream and a small spoonful of the reserved pesto.

Scatter over a few oregano leaves and serve with the crunchy toasted sourdough.

pork & kale soup

Serves 4

When we were filming 'Junior MasterChef', a lovely young contestant called Te Ani made this delicious, soulful Maori soup. I loved it so much that I snuck into the kitchen and tracked it down for my dinner. Eating this soup in my sterile hotel room made me feel like I was back at home.

METHOD

Prepare your pork belly strips by removing the skin (if it is still attached) with a sharp knife, then cutting the belly into 3 cm (1¼ inch) cubes.

Heat the olive oil in a large heavy-based saucepan over medium heat. Add the onion, garlic and bacon and cook for about 5 minutes, or until the onion has softened.

Add the fennel seeds (if using), pork belly and ribs and cook for 2 more minutes, or until the meat is lightly sealed but not browned.

Pour in the stock and water and bring to the boil, then reduce the heat to low and simmer for 30–40 minutes or until the meat is tender.

Remove the pork ribs and discard.

Increase the heat to medium–high, add the kale and cook for about 5 minutes, or until the kale starts to wilt.

Season with salt and pepper, divide between bowls and serve with the grilled sourdough.

INGREDIENTS

600 g (1 lb 5 oz) boneless
    pork belly strips, about 3 cm
    (1¼ inches) thick
1 tablespoon olive oil
2 small brown onions, finely
    chopped
3 garlic cloves, minced
2 bacon slices, finely chopped
2 teaspoons fennel seeds (optional)
350 g (12 oz) lean pork ribs, cut
    into individual bones (ask
    your butcher to do this for you)
2 litres (70 fl oz/8 cups) good-
    quality chicken stock
250 ml (9 fl oz/1 cup) water
6–8 kale or silverbeet (Swiss
    chard) stalks, leaves stripped,
    washed and shredded
sea salt and freshly ground
    black pepper
4 slices of sourdough
    bread, grilled, to serve

chicken, pork & green bean terrine

Serves 10–12

I used to be scared of making terrines, but when I finally mustered up the courage I was so surprised by how easy they were to master. The great thing about terrines is that you can make them the day before and they are posh, portable and super impressive!

INGREDIENTS

20 g (¾ oz) butter

1 small brown onion, finely chopped

4 garlic cloves, finely chopped

80 g (2¾ oz) chicken livers, cleaned and roughly chopped

big splash of Cognac

300 g (10½ oz) skinless, boneless chicken thigh fillets (about 2) (free-range or organic, if you can), excess fat trimmed and each cut into thirds

400 g (14 oz) skinless chicken breast fillets (free-range or organic, if you can), diced

250 g (9 oz) minced (ground) pork

100 g (3½ oz) baby spinach, chopped

45 g (1½ oz/¾ cup lightly packed) fresh breadcrumbs (made from day-old bread)

3 teaspoons drained green peppercorns in brine

135 g (4¾ oz/1 cup) hazelnuts, roasted and peeled

2 sage leaves, thinly sliced

1 teaspoon thyme leaves, finely chopped

2 teaspoons marjoram leaves, finely chopped

finely grated zest of 1 lemon

1½ teaspoons sea salt

freshly ground black pepper

1 egg, lightly beaten

250 g (9 oz) thinly sliced prosciutto (rindless but with lots of fat), sliced lengthways

10 baby green beans, trimmed

crusty bread, to serve

red capsicum (pepper) relish, to serve

METHOD

Preheat the oven to 180°C (350°F/Gas 4).

Melt the butter in a medium frying pan over low heat.

Add the onion and garlic and cook for 5–6 minutes, or until the onion has softened. Increase the heat to medium, add the livers and cook for 1 minute. Add the Cognac and cook for 30 seconds.

Transfer the mixture to a large bowl and allow to cool.

Add the remaining terrine ingredients (except the prosciutto and beans) to the bowl and combine well.

Line the base and two long sides of a 28 x 8 x 8 cm (11¼ x 3¼ x 3¼ inch), 1.75 litre (61 fl oz/7 cup) capacity terrine dish with baking paper, making sure the paper hangs over the sides.

Carefully line the base and sides of the terrine dish with the slices of prosciutto. Make sure they are slightly overlapping so there are no gaps and there is enough hanging over the sides to fold back over the top.

Scoop one-third of the mixture into the dish and randomly top with five of the green beans lengthways. Top with half of the remaining mixture and the remaining beans. Top with the remaining mixture and press down to flatten.

Fold the overhanging prosciutto back over the flattened mixture, then fold over the overhanging baking paper to completely enclose the terrine.

Put the terrine dish into a large ovenproof dish and pour in enough hot water to reach halfway up the terrine dish. Bake for about 1 hour, or until the terrine is firm to the touch.

Remove from the water bath and allow to cool, then refrigerate overnight with a weight placed on top of the terrine (I use a brick or a few tins of tomatoes).

Turn the terrine out onto a serving platter and serve with some crusty bread and red capsicum relish.

black & white pepper duck salad with spiced tamarillo

Serves 4

Tamarillos and duck have a perfect relationship; they bring the best out in each other. If you have time, it's a great idea to poach the tamarillos the day before serving and refrigerate overnight — they will turn a blushing bright red and the flavours will really develop. This salad also works nicely with the dressing from the quail recipe on page 52.

INGREDIENTS

4 medium duck breasts
1 tablespoon whole black peppercorns, coarsely ground
1 tablespoon whole white peppercorns, coarsely ground
1 teaspoon sea salt
drizzle of olive oil

POACHED SPICED TAMARILLOS

165 g ($5\frac{3}{4}$ oz/$\frac{3}{4}$ cup) caster (superfine) sugar
375 ml (13 fl oz/$1\frac{1}{2}$ cups) water
juice of 1 orange and 1 strip of zest
1 whole star anise
2 cardamom pods, bruised
$\frac{1}{2}$ teaspoon sea salt
6 red tamarillos (see Note)

DRESSING

170 ml ($5\frac{1}{2}$ fl oz/$\frac{2}{3}$ cup) tamarillo-poaching syrup (see left)
80 ml ($2\frac{1}{2}$ fl oz/$\frac{1}{3}$ cup) olive oil
sea salt and freshly ground black pepper

SALAD

1 purple witlof (chicory), leaves separated
1 white witlof (chicory), leaves separated
120 g ($4\frac{1}{4}$ oz/2 cups) snow peas (mangetout) sprouts
30 g (1 oz/1 cup) baby watercress or micro herbs
1 baby cos (romaine) heart, leaves separated
3 spring onions (scallions), each cut into 3 lengths and thinly sliced
2 Lebanese (short) cucumbers, halved lengthways and thinly sliced
120 g ($4\frac{1}{4}$ oz) snow peas (mangetout), stringed and blanched

METHOD

Preheat the oven to 200°C (400°F/Gas 6).

TO MAKE THE POACHED SPICED TAMARILLOS

Put the sugar, water, orange juice and zest, star anise, cardamom and salt in a small saucepan over medium heat and simmer for about 10 minutes, or until the sugar has dissolved and the flavours have infused.

Make a criss-cross slit at the top of each tamarillo and remove the stem. Simmer in the syrup for about 10 minutes, or until just tender.

Remove the pan from the heat, scoop out the tamarillos and leave to cool.

Carefully peel and discard the tamarillo skins once they are cool enough to handle.

Return the four prettiest ones to the syrup.

Roughly chop the remaining two and add back to the syrup for extra colour. Set aside until serving.

TO COOK THE DUCK BREASTS

Pat the duck breasts dry with paper towel. Scatter the ground black and white peppercorns evenly over a large plate, then sprinkle over the salt. Generously coat the skin side of each breast in the salt and pepper mixture, then turn over and lightly coat the flesh side.

Heat the olive oil in a large non-stick ovenproof frying pan over low heat. Once hot, cook the duck, skin side down, for 8–10 minutes, or until the skin is crispy and golden and the fat has rendered out.

Drain the duck fat from the pan, turn the breasts over and transfer the pan to the oven to finish cooking for about 4 minutes for medium (still a little pink inside), or until cooked to your liking.

Rest for a few minutes before slicing.

TO MAKE THE DRESSING

Whisk all of the ingredients together and season with salt and pepper.

TO SERVE

Gently toss all of the salad ingredients together, arrange on four plates and drizzle some of the dressing over each salad.

Cut the whole tamarillos in half lengthways and place on the plates.

Place a sliced duck breast on top of each salad, and spoon over some of the tamarillo syrup.

NOTE If tamarillos are out of season you can substitute them with oranges, blood oranges or pink grapefruits. Just skip the poaching step and replace the poaching liquid in the dressing with citrus juice balanced with sugar or honey.

zucchini, feta & prosciutto linguini

Serves 4

When I run out of steam at the end of the week I often make a simple pasta. This one is light and luscious, and full of rich flavours.

METHOD

Cook the pasta in a large saucepan of lightly salted boiling water until *al dente* then drain. If your pasta is ready before your sauce, toss a little olive oil through the linguini to stop it from sticking together.

Heat the olive oil in a wok over low heat.

Add the garlic and stir for about 1 minute, being careful not to let it burn.

Add the zucchini and lemon zest and cook, tossing for about 2 minutes, or until the zucchini softens a little.

Add the marjoram, dill, butter and lemon juice and stir to combine.

Add the drained pasta to the wok and combine.

Toss in the feta, prosciutto and parsley and season with salt and pepper.

Serve immediately with a gorgeous green salad.

INGREDIENTS

500 g (1 lb 2 oz) linguini

80 ml (2½ fl oz/⅓ cup) olive oil, plus extra for drizzling, if needed

8 garlic cloves, finely chopped

2 zucchini (courgettes), very thinly sliced (I use a mandoline)

finely grated zest and juice of 1 lemon

¼ cup marjoram leaves

¼ cup dill sprigs

20 g (¾ oz) unsalted butter

200 g (7 oz) feta cheese (Danish feta is ideal), crumbled

100 g (3½ oz) thinly sliced prosciutto, cut into thin strips

¼ cup flat-leaf (Italian) parsley leaves, chopped

sea salt and freshly ground black pepper

grapevine lamb loaf

Serves 8

I dedicate this dish to my mum because, as a '70s kid, I was born and bred on meatloaf. This is my glammed-up version with the addition of Mediterranean flavours. It is delicious served with harissa and minted yoghurt.

INGREDIENTS

1 tablespoon olive oil, plus extra
    for greasing
1 large brown onion, finely diced
3 garlic cloves, finely diced
⅓ cup finely diced preserved
    lemon (I use the skin and
    the flesh)
2 teaspoons ground coriander
3 teaspoons ground cumin
1 teaspoon ground cinnamon
80 g (2¾ oz/½ cup) pine nuts, toasted
1 cup coriander (cilantro) leaves,
    finely chopped
⅓ cup mint leaves, finely chopped
750 g (1 lb 10 oz) lean minced
    (ground) lamb
280 g (10 oz/1½ cups) cooked
    brown rice (110 g/3¾ oz/½ cup
    uncooked brown rice)
¼ cup vine leaves in brine,
    drained and finely chopped
1 egg
½ teaspoon sea salt
freshly ground black pepper
20–30 whole vine leaves, for
    lining the tin

METHOD

Preheat the oven to 180°C (350°F/Gas 4).

Heat the olive oil in a small frying pan over low–medium heat. Add the onion and garlic and cook for about 5 minutes, or until the onion is translucent. Remove and put in a large bowl.

Add all of the remaining ingredients (except the whole vine leaves) to the bowl and combine well.

Rinse the whole vine leaves in cold water to remove their saltiness, then pat dry with paper towel.

Lightly grease a 1.25 litre (44 fl oz/5 cup) capacity loaf (bar) tin or terrine dish and carefully line the base and sides with slightly overlapping vine leaves, making sure there are no gaps. Allow the vine leaves to hang over the sides and reserve some leaves for covering the top later.

Spread the lamb mixture evenly in the tin and pat down firmly with your hands. Cover the top with the reserved leaves and neatly fold over the overhanging ones. Cover with a lid or wrap tightly with foil.

Put the tin in an ovenproof dish and pour in enough hot water to reach halfway up the tin.

Bake for 1 hour, then remove from the water bath and allow to cool.

Refrigerate for a few hours, or overnight, with a weight on top (I use a brick or tinned tomatoes).

Slice and serve with lashings of harissa and minted yoghurt (see page 70).

chicken caesar salad with quail eggs

Serves 4

The mighty caesar salad has maintained its popularity as a staple on lunchtime menus all around the world. You can almost judge a restaurant by its take on this classic dish. I like to serve mine on a flat plate with all the pretty bits on top rather than toss everything together in a bowl.

INGREDIENTS

1 lemon, thinly sliced into rounds

a few rosemary sprigs

a few thyme sprigs

2 large skinless chicken breast fillets (free-range or organic, if you can)

drizzle of olive oil

juice of $\frac{1}{2}$ a lemon

sea salt and freshly ground black pepper

1 ciabatta roll (or an 8 cm/3¼ inch thick slice from a loaf), frozen (to make slicing easier)

25 g (1 oz) butter, melted

20 thin slices pancetta

100 g (3½ oz) baby cos (romaine) lettuce leaves (preferably from the heart) or baby spinach leaves

6 anchovy fillets (optional), halved lengthways

10 quail eggs, soft-boiled, peeled and halved (see Note)

shaved parmesan cheese, to garnish

DRESSING

2 egg yolks, at room temperature

1 garlic clove, minced

2 teaspoons dijon mustard

1 tablespoon tarragon vinegar

1 tablespoon lemon juice

5 anchovy fillets

185 ml (6 fl oz/¾ cup) mild olive oil

2 tablespoons hot water

2 teaspoons worcestershire sauce

1 heaped tablespoon grated parmesan cheese

pinch of sea salt

METHOD

Preheat the oven to 190°C (375°F/Gas 5).

Scatter the lemon slices and herbs in the middle of a baking tray and put the chicken directly on top.

Drizzle over the olive oil and lemon juice, season with salt and pepper then cover tightly with foil so no steam can escape.

Bake for 25–30 minutes, depending on the thickness of the fillets, or until just cooked through.

Remove from the oven and reduce the temperature to 160°C (315°F/Gas 2–3).

TO MAKE THE DRESSING

Blitz the egg yolks, garlic, mustard, vinegar, lemon juice and anchovies in a small food processor until well combined.

Slowly drizzle in the olive oil with the processor still running and blend until the mixture is smooth and has thickened.

Add the water, 1 tablespoon at a time, then add the worcestershire sauce, parmesan and salt. Turn off the processor, taste for seasoning then transfer to a bowl and set aside.

TO MAKE CROÛTONS AND ROAST THE PANCETTA

Cut the ciabatta into wafer-thin slices. Lightly brush a baking tray with some of the melted butter. Arrange the ciabatta slices on the tray, generously brush with the remaining butter and sprinkle with salt and pepper.

Bake for 10–15 minutes, or until light golden.

Arrange the pancetta slices on a baking tray lined with baking paper. Cover with another sheet of baking paper and press down. This will keep the pancetta flat.

Bake for about 10 minutes, or until crisp.

TO ASSEMBLE

Smear spoonfuls of the dressing in perfect circles over the bases of four dinner plates.

Place a few cos lettuce leaves on top.

Slice the chicken thinly and arrange on top.

Scatter a few more lettuce leaves in any gaps.

Arrange the croûtons, crispy pancetta, anchovies, halved quail eggs and parmesan shavings over the top and drizzle over the remaining dressing.

Enjoy while the chicken is still warm and juicy.

NOTE To soft-boil quail eggs, put them in a pan, cover with cold water and bring to the boil over high heat. Once boiling, cook the eggs for $1\frac{1}{2}$ minutes, then drain and refresh them immediately in ice-cold water. Be careful when peeling them as they are very delicate!

pretty frittata

Serves 4–6

A frittata is basically a pastry-free quiche cooked in a pan like a pie, and loaded up with a variety of veggies or whatever takes your fancy. It's a great way to use up leftovers! I call this 'pretty frittata' because it's colourful, crunchy and tasty.

METHOD

Preheat the oven to 180°C (350°F/Gas 4).

Roast the capsicums for about 30 minutes, or until the skin slightly blackens and blisters.

Remove from the oven, put in a bowl then cover with plastic wrap and allow to cool. Peel off the skins, discard the seeds and finely chop the flesh.

Toss the sweet potato with the olive oil, salt and pepper. Arrange in a single layer on two large non-stick baking trays and roast for about 20 minutes, or until almost cooked through.

Melt the butter in a frying pan over low heat. Add the leek and garlic and cook for 6–8 minutes, or until the leek has softened.

Whisk the eggs, cream, parmesan and dill together, and season with salt and pepper.

Lightly grease a 30 cm (12 inch) ovenproof frying pan or baking dish with butter and cover the base with the sweet potato. Spread the leek mixture evenly on top, then pour over the egg mixture. Evenly scatter over the spinach and roasted capsicum, then sprinkle over the sunflower seeds.

Bake for 30 minutes, or until set, and serve hot or cold.

INGREDIENTS

2 red capsicums (peppers)

600 g (1 lb 5 oz) sweet potatoes, peeled and cut into 5 mm (¼ inch) thick slices

drizzle of olive oil

sea salt and freshly ground black pepper

30 g (1 oz) unsalted butter, plus extra for greasing

1 leek, white part only, thinly sliced

2 garlic cloves, finely chopped

7 eggs

300 ml (10½ fl oz) thin (pouring) cream

50 g (1¾ oz/⅓ cup) finely grated parmesan cheese

½ cup chopped dill

180 g (about 6½ oz/1 bunch) English spinach, leaves washed, blanched and squeezed dry

55 g (2 oz/⅓ cup) sunflower seeds

quail with pistachio, orange & sage butter

Serves 4

One delicious little quail would certainly leave me ravenous at dinnertime. They are, however, perfect for a 'ladies' light lunch'. This dish screams of summertime to me. I like to serve it with a fresh fig, rocket and fennel salad.

INGREDIENTS

4 quail
2 teaspoons finely grated orange zest
45 g (1½ oz/⅓ cup) pistachio nut kernels, finely chopped
8 sage leaves, finely chopped
40 g (1½ oz) unsalted butter, at room temperature
sea salt and freshly ground black pepper
olive oil, for frying

DRESSING

60 ml (2 fl oz/¼ cup) freshly squeezed orange juice
60 ml (2 fl oz/¼ cup) extra virgin olive oil
1 garlic clove, minced
sea salt and freshly ground black pepper

SALAD

½ red onion, thinly sliced
1 fennel bulb, thinly shaved
4 fresh figs, quartered
100 g (3½ oz/2¾ cups, tightly packed) rocket (arugula)

METHOD

Preheat the oven to 200°C (400°F/Gas 6).

Partially debone each quail. To do this, cut down and along both sides of the spine from the neck to the tail with a pair of kitchen scissors, then remove and discard the spine.

Flatten each quail out. Use a small sharp knife to cut under the rib bones and remove them as well. Put the quail, skin side up, on a chopping board and press firmly down on each to completely flatten.

Combine the orange zest, pistachios, sage, butter, salt and pepper in a small bowl to form a paste. Divide the paste into four portions.

Carefully lift the skin at the neck end of each quail and push a portion of the paste under the skin, spreading it evenly over the flesh and keeping the skin intact.

Heat a few splashes of olive oil in a large ovenproof frying pan over medium heat. Add the quail, flesh side down, and cook for 3–4 minutes, then turn over and cook the skin side for 3–4 minutes, or until crispy.

Transfer the pan to the oven and roast the quail for 4–5 minutes to finish cooking.

Remove from the oven and allow to rest, flesh side down, for 5 minutes.

TO MAKE THE DRESSING

Whisk the orange juice, olive oil and garlic together in a bowl and season with salt and pepper.

TO MAKE THE SALAD

Combine the onion, fennel, fig and rocket in a bowl.

Dress the salad just before serving, and divide between your plates.

Place a quail on each plate, next to the salad. Drizzle over any resting juices then serve.

hot-smoked salmon
& quinoa salad

Serves 4–6

Sometimes a heavy lunch can stop you in your tracks. This super-food salad is light, delicious and will leave you feeling energised enough to swing from the chandeliers! If you don't fancy a hot-pink salad, add the beetroot after you've tossed the other ingredients together.

INGREDIENTS

250 g (9 oz) sweet potato, peeled and
    cut into 2 cm (¾ inch) cubes
drizzle of olive oil
sea salt and freshly ground black pepper
200 g (7 oz/1 cup) quinoa (see Note)
500 ml (17 fl oz/2 cups) water
250 g (9 oz) baby beetroot (beets), trimmed
    but unpeeled
1 small fennel bulb, thinly shaved
½ small red onion, thinly sliced
50 g (1¾ oz) sunflower sprouts or micro herbs
1 small bunch of flat-leaf (Italian) parsley
    leaves picked and roughly chopped
1 small bunch of dill, roughly chopped
100 g (3½ oz) soft goat's feta cheese or curd
250 g (9 oz) piece of hot-smoked salmon,
    skin and bones removed, flaked
1 lemon, cut into wedges, to serve

DRESSING

60 ml (2 fl oz/¼ cup) extra virgin olive oil
60 ml (2 fl oz/¼ cup) freshly squeezed
    lemon juice
sea salt and freshly ground black pepper

METHOD

Preheat the oven to 200°C (400°F/Gas 6).

Put the sweet potato in a roasting tray, drizzle with the olive oil, season with salt and pepper and toss to coat well.

Bake for about 20 minutes, or until tender, then allow to cool.

Meanwhile, wash and strain the quinoa then put it in a medium saucepan with the water and a pinch of salt, and bring to the boil over medium–high heat.

Reduce the heat to low and simmer, uncovered, for 10 minutes. After that, cover with a lid and simmer for 5 minutes.

Turn off the heat and allow to cool.

Steam the beetroot for about 20 minutes, or until they can be easily pierced with a fork.

Peel off the beetroot skins under cold running water (wear rubber gloves if you don't want pink hands) and cut into wedges.

TO MAKE THE DRESSING

Put the extra virgin olive oil and lemon juice in a bowl, season with salt and pepper and whisk to combine.

TO MAKE THE SALAD

Combine the cooked sweet potato, quinoa, fennel, onion, sprouts, herbs and half of the dressing in a large bowl, then divide the salad between the serving bowls, and top each with a few wedges of beetroot.

Break up the goat's feta with your fingers and scatter over the salads. Top with large flakes of salmon, drizzle over the rest of the dressing and serve immediately with wedges of lemon for squeezing over.

NOTE I often use the white quinoa for this salad, but it also works well with a mixture of red, white and black quinoa.

feeding family & friends

I have never been dropped by a friend via text or unfriended on Facebook. Nor have I serenaded a lover or brawled in a bar. You will know how I feel about you when I cook for you. Wrong me, and dine on boot-leather lasagne! Love me, and you'll find your taste buds flashdancing in your mouth to funky soul music. Spoiling my friends and family with food is an absolute joy for me. I adore the spontaneity of whipping up something quick and fancy, and I thrive on the seduction of cooking something slow and yummy for the people I love. The by-products of a house full of beautiful smells and warmth are like getting $10 change from a $5 note. Sitting down with my family and friends to enjoy a meal is when I feel most at home. These are some of my favourite ways to tell people I love them.

two-minute steaks with salsa picante

Serves 4–6

Prepare your salsa first as the steaks take no time at all. You will need to get two pans on the go for this one, and if you're feeding a crowd just double the quantities and cook the steaks on the barbecue.

INGREDIENTS

14 thin slices trimmed beef
    scotch or eye fillet (ask your
    butcher to cut these like
    minute steaks for you)
60 ml (2 fl oz/¼ cup) olive oil
1 tablespoon thyme leaves
sea salt and freshly ground
    black pepper

SALSA PICANTE

¼ cup flat-leaf (Italian) parsley
    leaves, finely chopped
50 g (1¾ oz/¼ cup) tiny capers,
    rinsed and finely chopped
1 garlic clove, finely chopped
1 small red chilli, seeded and
    finely chopped
¼ cup finely diced red onion
60 ml (2 fl oz/¼ cup) freshly
    squeezed lemon juice
60 ml (2 fl oz/¼ cup) olive oil
½ teaspoon sea salt
1 teaspoon soft brown sugar

TO MAKE THE SALSA PICANTE

Combine all of the ingredients in a small bowl then taste to check for a good balance of sweet, sour and salty flavours.
Set aside until serving.

TO PREPARE AND COOK THE STEAKS

Bash the steaks with a meat mallet until they are very thin.
Rub the steaks with the olive oil, thyme, salt and pepper.
Heat two large heavy-based frying pans over high heat or a barbecue hotplate set to high.
Cook the steaks for 1 minute on each side.
Fan out the steaks on a large serving platter and spoon over the salsa picante.
Eat immediately with a lovely fresh salad (see Note).

NOTE This is yummy with the quick artichoke and spinach salad on page 109 and also the fennel salad on page 106.

paella for fifteen

Serves a party

I love a dish that becomes the reason for a gathering, and paella is a great example of such a dish. It's one of my favourite party tricks, and I love to cook it outside among the crowd as it's a great spectators' dish. The secret to a good paella is making sure all of the ingredients are cooked perfectly in time with the rice — this means pre-cooking some of them, which also seasons the pan with great flavour.

This recipe calls for a 55 cm (22 inch) paella pan. I invested in one a few years ago with a fitted gas burner and it's been fantastic. It's so portable that I've even cooked paella on a wheelbarrow in the middle of a paddock! If you don't have a burner big enough, you can put the pan on a barbecue hotplate to ensure even cooking. I usually do all my prep and seal off the meat and veg before the guests arrive so all the messy stuff is out of the way. Once the guests arrive, it's plain sailing and I need only fry up the aromatics and rice, scatter over the ingredients and add the stock. Whatever you do, don't stir it; it will cook itself and have everyone drooling!

INGREDIENTS

olive oil, for cooking

800 g (1 lb 12 oz) fresh chorizo, cut into 1–2 cm ($\frac{1}{2}$–$\frac{3}{4}$ inch) thick slices

600 g (1 lb 5 oz) raw tiger prawns (shrimp), peeled with tails left on

3 litres (105 fl oz/12 cups) hot, good-quality chicken stock

1 teaspoon saffron threads

1.5 kg (3 lb 5 oz) skinless, boneless chicken thigh fillets (free-range or organic, if you can), excess fat trimmed and cut into 4–5 cm (1$\frac{1}{2}$–2 inch) pieces

1 tablespoon smoked hot paprika

3 red capsicums (peppers), cut into 2 cm ($\frac{3}{4}$ inch) pieces

600 g (1 lb 5 oz) green beans, trimmed and cut into 3 cm (1$\frac{1}{4}$ inch) lengths

1 x 240 g (8$\frac{1}{2}$ oz) tin of artichokes in brine or oil, drained and halved

3 red onions, finely diced

3–4 red bird's eye chillies, finely chopped

10 garlic cloves, finely chopped

1 bunch of thyme, leaves stripped

1.32 kg (3 lb/6 cups) Spanish paella rice or risotto rice

375 ml (13 fl oz/1$\frac{1}{2}$ cups) dry white wine

40 black mussels, scrubbed and debearded

lemon wedges, to serve

METHOD

Heat a big splash of olive oil in a 55 cm (22 inch) paella pan over high heat. Add the chorizo and prawns and cook for 2–3 minutes to just seal. Remove and put into a bowl.

Heat the chicken stock in a large saucepan until it reaches boiling point, then add the saffron threads, reduce to a low heat and simmer gently until needed.

Dust the chicken in the paprika then add it to the paella pan with a little more oil, if needed, and fry until half cooked. Remove and put into a separate bowl.

Add the capsicums, beans and artichokes to the paella pan and cook for a few minutes, or until the vegetables start to slightly char and take on a smoky aroma. Remove and put into a third bowl, separate from the meat.

Coat the paella pan with a little more oil, reduce the heat to medium and lightly cook the onion, chilli, garlic and thyme for a few minutes, or until the onions start to soften.

Add the rice and stir for 2 minutes to coat it in the flavours.

Reduce the heat to low, spread the rice evenly over the base of the pan, then layer the pre-cooked ingredients on top. I always start with the chicken to ensure the meat gets cooked all the way through, then the veggies, followed by the chorizo and prawns.

Pour over the wine and most of the hot stock (including the saffron), reserving 250 ml (9 fl oz/1 cup) to add towards the end if needed.

Simmer, without stirring, for 10 minutes.

Arrange the mussels over the top and simmer for a further 15 minutes, without stirring. If the rice is not *al dente* and all the liquid has been absorbed, add the reserved stock and cook for a few more minutes.

Turn off the heat, cover the entire pan with foil and let the paella sit for 5 minutes so those Spanish flavours can work their flamenco magic.

Serve with the lemon wedges.

whole poached trout with celeriac rémoulade

Serves 8–10

You don't need a fish poacher to poach a fish. I'm a big believer in having multipurpose kitchen equipment, so for this recipe all you need is a large roasting tray — if you lay the fish diagonally across the base, it should fit perfectly. This is a nice, healthy way to cook fish, and it deserves a slightly naughty side serve of celeriac rémoulade.

INGREDIENTS

1.5 kg (3 lb 5 oz) whole ocean
    trout, scaled and gutted
small handful of tarragon leaves,
    to garnish (optional)

POACHING STOCK

1 tablespoon olive oil
1 brown onion, finely chopped
2 sticks of celery, finely chopped, or any
    trimmings and stalks from the celeriac
    (celery root) (see rémoulade)
70 g (2½ oz/½ cup) finely chopped fennel
50 g (1¾ oz/½ cup) thinly sliced leek, white
    part only
25 g (1 oz/¼ cup) thinly sliced mushrooms,
    or mushroom skins
2 garlic cloves, finely chopped
1 fresh bay leaf
3 litres (105 fl oz/12 cups) water
sea salt and freshly ground
    black pepper

CELERIAC RÉMOULADE

1 small celeriac (celery root)
juice of ½ a lemon
1 teaspoon sea salt
60 g (2¼ oz/¼ cup) good-quality mayonnaise
80 ml (2½ fl oz/⅓ cup) thin (pouring) cream
1 teaspoon dijon mustard
drizzle of worcestershire sauce

TO POACH THE FISH

Heat the olive oil in a large saucepan over low heat. Add the vegetables, garlic and bay leaf and cook for about 10 minutes to bring out all the flavours.

Add the water and season with salt and pepper. Simmer for 20 minutes to allow the flavours to infuse.

Lay the trout diagonally across the base of a large, deep flameproof roasting tray then pour the poaching stock into the tray so it comes halfway up the trout.

Put the tray over medium heat and bring the stock back to a gentle boil, then turn the trout over.

Cover the tray with foil, sealing the edges well so the steam can't escape, and cook for another 2–3 minutes, or until the stock starts to boil again. Turn off the heat and leave the trout to gently poach in the stock as it cools to room temperature (about 25–30 minutes).

Carefully remove the trout to a serving platter and allow it to rest for 30 minutes.

TO MAKE THE CELERIAC RÉMOULADE

Peel and grate the celeriac (you'll get the best results using a mandoline).

Combine well with the lemon juice and salt.

Mix the mayonnaise, cream, mustard and worcestershire sauce in another bowl.

Add the mayonnaise mixture to the celeriac and stir to coat well. Set aside until serving.

TO SERVE

Peel the skin from the fish (it should come away easily), leaving the head and tail intact.

Brush the trout with any resting juices to seal it and give it a nice shine, then garnish as desired (I like to use tarragon leaves).

Serve with the celeriac rémoulade.

spiced lamb chops

Serves 6–8

Lamb is such sweet meat, and it lends itself beautifully to whatever you throw at it. This is a blend of my favourite spices to dress up lamb chops and get them ready for a party. This combination of spices also works beautifully with one whole deboned flattened lamb leg on the barbecue.

TO MAKE THE SPICE PASTE

Lightly toast the cumin and coriander seeds in a small dry frying pan over medium heat until fragrant.
Transfer to a mortar, add the cloves, cinnamon stick and salt and pound until fine with a pestle.
Stir in the remaining ingredients until a paste forms.

TO COOK THE LAMB CHOPS

Preheat a barbecue to medium–high.
Rub the spice paste all over the chops and barbecue for 4–5 minutes each side for medium-rare, or until cooked to your liking.
Serve with lemon wedges and a salad. Any of these three veggie dishes would be lovely with these chops: roasted tomato and chickpea salad (see page 96), quinoa tabouleh (see page 110) or the dukkah-spiced eggplant recipe (see page 114).

INGREDIENTS

20 lamb loin chops
lemon wedges, to serve

SPICE PASTE

30 g (1 oz) cumin seeds
2 tablespoons coriander seeds
1 teaspoon whole cloves
½ a cinnamon stick
1 teaspoon sea salt
1 teaspoon cayenne pepper
1 teaspoon ground turmeric
5 garlic cloves, minced
1 red chilli, finely chopped
80 ml (2½ fl oz/⅓ cup) olive oil

chermoula chicken with harissa & minted yoghurt

Serves 6

You can buy pre-made condiments and marinades from your local grocery or gourmet food store, but I love to start from scratch and make my own, especially when it comes to harissa and chermoula pastes. The roasting and grinding of the spices make the house smell amazing and aromatic, and the outcome is so rewarding. This recipe was inspired by my wonderful food friend, Ursula Nairn. She's the unsung hero in all of my television cooking shows ... always behind the scenes working her magic.

INGREDIENTS
12–14 plump skinless, boneless chicken
    thigh fillets (free-range or organic,
    if you can), excess fat trimmed
drizzle of olive oil

HARISSA
2 tablespoons cumin seeds
2 tablespoons coriander seeds
3 big red capsicums (peppers), roasted,
    peeled and seeded
1 long red chilli, chopped (extra if you
    like it hot)
2 garlic cloves
½ teaspoon sea salt
½ teaspoon sugar
80 ml (2½ fl oz/⅓ cup) vegetable oil

CHERMOULA MARINADE
½ cup harissa (see left)
½ cup chopped flat-leaf (Italian) parsley
¼ cup chopped mint
¾ cup chopped coriander (cilantro) leaves
    and stems
3 garlic cloves, chopped
½ teaspoon ground cinnamon
¾ of a preserved lemon (I use the skin and
    flesh) (see Note)
60 ml (2 fl oz/¼ cup) vegetable oil
sea salt and freshly ground black pepper

MINTED YOGHURT
pinch of sugar
pinch of sea salt
juice of ½ a lemon
5 mint leaves, thinly sliced
130 g (4½ oz/½ cup) thick Greek-style yoghurt

TO MAKE THE HARISSA

Toast the cumin and coriander seeds in a small dry frying pan over medium heat for a few minutes, or until fragrant. Be careful not to burn them or they will taste bitter.
Transfer to a mortar and grind with a pestle until very fine.
Blitz the pounded spices, capsicum, chilli, garlic, salt and sugar in a blender until smooth.
Leave the blender running and slowly drizzle in the vegetable oil until the mixture is thick and luscious. Taste to test the chilli factor and seasoning, and adjust if needed.
Spoon some of the harissa into a bowl, leaving a ½ cup of it in the blender for the chermoula marinade, and refrigerate until needed.

TO MAKE THE CHERMOULA MARINADE

Add all of the marinade ingredients to the blender with the harissa and blitz until smooth. Taste and add salt only if it needs it (remember that the preserved lemon is already salty).

TO MAKE THE MINTED YOGHURT

Combine the sugar, salt and lemon juice in a small bowl, then stir in the mint and yoghurt. Refrigerate until needed.

TO PREPARE AND SERVE

Put the chicken in a large bowl, add the marinade and toss to coat well.
Cover and refrigerate for at least 1 hour.
Preheat the oven to 180°C (350°F/Gas 4).
Heat the olive oil in a large non-stick frying pan over high heat. Add the chicken in two batches, seal on both sides and then put in a large roasting tray.
Roast for 20–25 minutes, depending on the thickness of the fillets.
Serve the chicken on a platter with the harissa and minted yoghurt so everyone can help themselves. Delicious with the roasted veg couscous (see page 126), quinoa tabouleh (see page 110) or roasted sweet potatoes and parsnips.

NOTE You can replace the preserved lemon with the zest, juice and flesh of 1 lemon (but don't use the white pith, it will make it bitter). Just remember to add a couple of pinches of salt to the marinade to compensate for the saltiness of the preserved lemon.

mexican pulled-pork shoulder

Serves 15 easily

This is a great crowd pleaser. Don't be put off by the long list of ingredients. It mainly consists of herbs and spices, which I put together to achieve a magical Mexican flavour. This dish takes no time to prep, and it cooks slowly in the oven — warming up the kitchen and making it smell incredible. This will feed plenty of people, and the leftovers taste even better the next day. I usually serve this with tortillas or big baked potatoes, deconstructed guacamole (see page 99), shredded iceberg lettuce and sour cream. The best thing about this dish is that everyone helps themselves.

INGREDIENTS

60 ml (2 fl oz/¼ cup) olive oil

3 brown onions, diced

10 garlic cloves, finely chopped

2 green chillies, finely chopped

1 red chilli, finely chopped

3 teaspoons dried oregano

1 tablespoon coriander seeds

1 tablespoon cumin seeds

1 tablespoon fennel seeds

1 teaspoon white peppercorns

1 cinnamon stick

2 whole star anise

10 whole cloves

2.5–3 kg (5 lb 8 oz–6 lb 12 oz) piece of pork shoulder, bone in and skin removed

2 heaped teaspoons smoked hot or sweet paprika

400 ml (14 fl oz) dry white wine

1 litre (35 fl oz/4 cups) good-quality chicken stock

10 ripe tomatoes, roughly chopped

2 teaspoons sea salt

a few thyme sprigs

4 x 400 g (14 oz) tins of black beans, drained and rinsed

1 x 400 g (14 oz) tin of kidney beans, drained and rinsed (optional)

2 cups coriander (cilantro) leaves and stems, chopped

1 cup flat-leaf (Italian) parsley leaves, chopped

METHOD

Preheat the oven to 170°C (325°F/Gas 3) and arrange an oven rack on the middle shelf.

Heat the olive oil in a large heavy-based flameproof casserole dish over medium heat. Add the onion and garlic and cook for 5–6 minutes, or until softened.

Add all the chillies, the dried oregano and spices (except the paprika) and cook, stirring, for 1–2 minutes to release the flavours.

Add the pork and paprika, turn to coat in the flavours, and cook for a few minutes on each side. Pour in the wine and chicken stock, then add the tomato, salt and thyme, and cover with a tight-fitting lid.

Roast in the oven for $3\frac{1}{2}$ hours, or until the pork pulls off the bone easily.

Remove the pork from the dish and pull the meat off the bone using two forks (discard the bone). Return the pulled pork to the sauce and add all of the beans.

Cook over medium heat for 20 minutes to heat the beans through and allow the flavours to mingle.

Stir through the coriander and parsley at the end and taste for seasoning before serving (this is beautiful with a dollop of sour cream and some diced avocado on top).

NOTE If you have any leftover pork and bean mix, make sure you save it for a hearty huevos rancheros (see page 14) the next morning.

slow-roasted pork belly

Serves 10

Four words that are dear to my heart: 'crispy crackling' and 'tender meat'. I think you can win just about anyone's heart with a perfectly roasted pork belly. It's a great way to feed a crowd because it roasts for over three hours, giving you plenty of time to run around the house and clean up before your guests arrive. Everyone seems to love pork, and the contrast of textures you get with pork belly is out of this world!

METHOD

Preheat the oven to 170°C (325°F/Gas 3).

Score the pork belly skin using a Stanley knife (or get your butcher to do it for you).

Fill a large flameproof roasting tray or pan that will fit the pork with 1 cm (½ inch) of water and bring to the boil over a high heat. Put the pork, skin side down, in the tray and cook for 1 minute then remove. This is the secret to really crispy skin.

Put the garlic, chopped rosemary, fennel seeds and salt in a mortar and grind to a paste with a pestle.

Rub the paste over the pork flesh, but not the skin.

Spread the vegetables and rosemary sprigs around the base of a large roasting tray and put the pork, skin side up, on top. Rub some salt into the skin.

Roast for 3 hours, or until tender.

Increase the oven temperature to 250°C (500°F/Gas 9) and roast for 30 minutes, or until the skin crackles up. Check the pork regularly so the skin doesn't burn. If the crackling is not as crisp as you would like it, put the pork under a hot grill (broiler) on a mid-to-low shelf and do not take your eyes off it while it's under the grill!

Serve with crispy roasted potatoes and a delicious salad such as Asian slaw (see page 102).

INGREDIENTS

- 2.5–3 kg (5 lb 8 oz–6 lb 12 oz) piece of pork belly (a few bones are okay), skin on
- 8 large garlic cloves
- 3 tablespoons finely chopped rosemary
- 3 tablespoons fennel seeds
- 2 teaspoons sea salt, plus extra for the pork skin
- 5 celery stalks
- 4 carrots, halved lengthways
- 2 large brown onions, quartered
- 4–5 long rosemary sprigs

nadia's cutleti

Makes 15–20

Every country has their version of a meat patty and *cutleti* is one of my favourites. My Ukrainian mother-in-law, Kateryna, introduced me to her mother Nadia's recipe. Cutleti are shaped like a prime cutlet without the bone. They are juicy, tasty and inexpensive, making them a great way to feed a big family. Whenever Kateryna invites us over for dinner and asks what we want to eat, we all say in unison, 'Cutleti!' For big gatherings, making the cutleti can become a social event in itself; many hands make light work.

INGREDIENTS

200 g (7 oz) sliced white bread, crusts removed
750 g (1 lb 10 oz) minced (ground) beef
250 g (9 oz) minced (ground) pork
2 brown onions, finely diced
120 g (4¼ oz/¾ cup) sunflower seeds, toasted
1 egg
1 teaspoon sea salt
freshly ground black pepper
180 g (6¼ oz/3 cups, lightly packed) fresh breadcrumbs (made from day-old bread)
sunflower oil, for shallow-frying

TOMATO SAUCE

60 ml (2 fl oz/¼ cup) olive oil
1 brown onion, finely chopped
5 garlic cloves, minced
8 ripe roma (plum) tomatoes, chopped
a handful of fresh mixed herbs (such as basil, thyme, rosemary or oregano), leaves roughly chopped
2 teaspoons sweet paprika
2 x 400 g (14 oz) tins chopped tomatoes
250 ml (9 fl oz/1 cup) water
1 dried bay leaf
1 teaspoon sugar
sea salt and freshly ground black pepper

TO MAKE THE CUTLETI

Cover the slices of bread with cold water and leave to soak until mushy.

Break up the bread with your clean fingers, squishing all the lumps to a fine consistency.

Squeeze out the excess water from the bread and put the bread in a large bowl.

Add the beef, pork, onion, sunflower seeds, egg, salt and pepper to the bowl. Combine well using your hands.

Take a handful of the mixture and cup it in the palm of your hand. Pat and press the mixture into a teardrop-shaped patty about 2.5 cm (1 inch) thick. You should get about 15–20 patties from the mixture, depending on the size of your hand.

Coat each patty generously in the breadcrumbs and lightly make a criss-cross pattern on each side with a knife. This helps the breadcrumbs to adhere and also helps the cutleti to crisp up.

Heat 125 ml (4 fl oz/½ cup) of sunflower oil in a large heavy-based frying pan over medium heat.

Cook the cutleti in three batches for a few minutes on each side, or until they are crispy and just cooked through. Reduce the heat if the cutleti start to burn and add more oil with each new batch, if needed.

Remove with a slotted spoon and drain on paper towel.

Serve the cutleti with the homemade tomato sauce, or anything else you like to have with meat patties.

TO MAKE THE TOMATO SAUCE

Heat the olive oil in a large heavy-based saucepan over medium heat. Add the onion and garlic and cook for 5 minutes, or until the onion is translucent.

Add the fresh tomato, herbs and paprika and cook for a few minutes.

Pour in the tinned tomatoes, water, bay leaf and sugar, then season with salt and pepper.

Reduce the heat to low and simmer for 20 minutes, or until the sauce has thickened a little and the flavours have mingled. Set aside until serving.

coq au vin blanc

Serves 8

This is one of my favourite classics from the '70s. I've poshed it up with some dried morels. If you can't get hold of morels, increase the quantity of button mushrooms. This is usually made with red wine, but I use white because it brightens the dish, plus it's a good excuse to open a bottle!

METHOD

Preheat the oven to 180°C (350°F/Gas 4).

Dust the chicken generously in flour, shaking off the excess.

Heat a generous amount of butter and olive oil in a large non-stick frying pan over medium–high heat.

Add the chicken thighs in batches, and cook until golden on both sides. Remove each cooked batch to a large casserole dish.

Deglaze the frying pan with half of the wine, then tip those wonderful juices into the casserole dish.

Add a little more butter and oil to the frying pan, gently cook the shallots until golden then transfer to the casserole dish.

Add the leek, garlic and pancetta to the frying pan and cook for a few minutes until the leek has softened.

Deglaze the pan with the remaining wine and Cognac (if using). Stand back in case it flames, then transfer everything to the casserole dish.

Add the remaining ingredients to the casserole dish, cover with a lid and cook for 1 hour.

Serve with steamed baby potatoes, baby carrots and green beans or sugarsnap peas.

INGREDIENTS

16 chicken thighs (free-range or organic, if you can), skin on and bone in

plain (all-purpose) flour, for dusting

butter and olive oil, for frying

500 ml (17 fl oz/2 cups) dry white wine

16 French shallots (eschalots) or pickling onions, peeled with roots left intact

2 leeks, white part only, thinly sliced

8 garlic cloves, sliced

160 g (5¾ oz) thinly sliced pancetta, sliced thinly

splash of Cognac (optional, but delicious)

350 g (12 oz) button mushrooms, halved

30 g (1 oz) dried morels, soaked in warm water for 20 minutes, then drained

1 litre (35 fl oz/4 cups) good-quality chicken stock

12 sage leaves

2 tablespoons tarragon leaves

2 tablespoons thyme leaves

3 fresh bay leaves

sea salt and freshly ground black pepper

flattened kashmiri chicken

Serves 8

When you bite into this chicken it's such a delicious experience because you get an explosion of spice, ginger and lemon, and then a burst of oozing, warm yoghurt with a crunchy nutty finish. It really does it for me.

INGREDIENTS

2 plump chickens (free-range or organic, if you can)
drizzle of lemon juice
drizzle of olive oil
sea salt

SPICE MIX

1 tablespoon cumin seeds, lightly toasted
2 teaspoons coriander seeds, lightly toasted
12 cardamom pods, husks removed
1 teaspoon ground cloves
40 g (1½ oz) piece of fresh ginger, peeled and finely chopped
8–10 garlic cloves, finely chopped
2 long red chillies, finely chopped

30 g (1 oz) piece of fresh turmeric, peeled and finely chopped (or 2 teaspoons ground)
2 cups coriander (cilantro) leaves and stems, finely chopped
125 ml (4 fl oz/½ cup) lemon juice
2 tablespoons vegetable oil
3 teaspoons sea salt

YOGHURT MIX

520 g (1 lb 2½ oz/2 cups) thick Greek-style yoghurt
160 g (5¾ oz/1 cup) whole almonds, roughly chopped
2 tablespoons honey

METHOD

Preheat the oven to 200°C (400°F/Gas 6).

TO MAKE THE SPICE MIX

Grind all of the dried spices to a fine powder using a mortar and pestle.

Transfer to a food processor and add the remaining ingredients. Blitz to a smooth paste then set aside.

TO MAKE THE YOGHURT MIX

Combine all of the ingredients in a bowl and set aside.

TO PREPARE AND COOK THE CHICKEN

Partially debone each chicken. To do this, cut down and along both sides of the spine from the neck to the parson's nose with a pair of kitchen scissors, then remove and discard the spine (or do as I do and save it to make stock).

Flatten each chicken out. Put a sheet of baking paper on top of the flattened chickens and, using a meat mallet or rolling pin, bang out the meat until it is evenly flat, being careful not to pierce the skin.

Spoon some of the spice mix under the skin, starting at the neck end of each chicken, and push it right down into the legs, spreading it evenly over the flesh and keeping the skin intact.

Spoon the yoghurt mix under the skin, spreading it evenly over the spice mix.

Put the chickens, skin side up, in a large non-stick roasting tray (or use a roasting tray lined with baking paper). Rub the outside of the chooks with a little lemon juice and olive oil then season with salt.

Cook for 30 minutes, then reduce the oven temperature to 170°C (325°F/Gas 3) and cook for another 25–30 minutes, or until cooked through. Baste the chooks with the tray juices every 10 minutes or so to keep them moist. If the basting juices are starting to dry out just add a tiny bit more water to the pan.

Carve each chicken into four pieces, reserve any resting juices for drizzling over, and serve with the warm chilli, pumpkin and lentil salad (see page 105) or a bowl of fluffy rice.

goat tagine

Serves 6

It's a mystery to me why people don't eat more goat because it's absolutely delicious. It's similar to lamb but less fatty, and a good butcher should be able to track down goat for you if he or she doesn't already stock it.

I cook this in a large heavy-based roasting tray or enamel casserole dish with a lid because I find most tagine dishes quite small. If you make it in a roasting tray, be sure to seal it well with baking paper and foil.

INGREDIENTS

1 kg (2 lb 4 oz) boneless goat shoulder,
    cut into 4 cm (1½ inch) pieces
1 goat or lamb front shank, cut into thirds
    (ask your butcher to do this)
olive oil, for cooking
400 g (14 oz) kipfler (fingerling) potatoes,
    halved lengthways
2 parsnips, each cut into 6 pieces
2 carrots, each cut into 3 pieces
12 French shallots (eschalots) or
    pickling onions
5 roma (plum) tomatoes, quartered
8 pitted prunes (optional)
1 strip of orange zest
1 strip of lemon zest
2 fresh bay leaves
1 cassia or cinnamon stick
600 ml (21 fl oz) good-quality chicken stock
2 x 400 g (14 oz) tins chickpeas (garbanzo
    beans), drained and rinsed

SPICE MIX

1½ teaspoons coriander seeds
3 cardamom pods, husks removed
3 whole cloves
3 teaspoons smoked hot paprika
½ teaspoon allspice
1 teaspoon sea salt
3 garlic cloves, chopped
1 long red chilli, chopped
10 g (¼ oz) piece of fresh ginger, peeled
    and chopped
2 tablespoons olive oil

TO SERVE

handful of chopped coriander (cilantro)
    leaves, to garnish
finely grated orange zest, to garnish
steamed couscous, to serve

TO MAKE THE SPICE MIX

Grind the coriander seeds, cardamom pods and cloves to a fine powder using a mortar and pestle.

Add the paprika, allspice, salt, garlic, chilli and ginger, pound to a paste and then stir in the olive oil.

TO PREPARE AND COOK THE GOAT

Rub the spice mix all over the goat and leave to marinate for 2 hours in the fridge.

Preheat the oven to 170°C (325°F/Gas 3).

Heat 1 tablespoon of olive oil in a heavy-based flameproof casserole dish or large tagine over medium heat. Add the potato, parsnip, carrot and shallots, and cook until light golden. Remove from the dish and set aside.

Heat a little more oil in the dish then add the marinated goat in two batches so the meat doesn't stew. Cook until lightly browned then remove from the dish and set aside, keeping it separate from the vegetables.

Return the cooked vegetables to the dish, then arrange the meat and the remaining ingredients (except the chickpeas, garnishes and couscous) on top. Cover and cook for 2½ hours, or until the goat is tender. Add the chickpeas for the last 30 minutes of cooking time.

Serve the tagine at the table with the coriander and orange zest scattered over, and a large bowl of couscous on the side.

peri peri fish & veggies

Serves 6

This is a one-tray wonder that can easily be doubled when you find yourself surrounded by hungry teenagers, or extra family members.

INGREDIENTS

6 firm white fish fillets
(about 200 g/7 oz each),
skinned and pinboned
small handful of coriander
(cilantro) leaves, to serve

VEGGIES

3 red onions
8–10 roma (plum) tomatoes
1 kg (2 lb 4 oz) potatoes, unpeeled
60 ml (2 fl oz/¼ cup) olive oil
2 tablespoons red wine vinegar
8 thyme sprigs
4 fresh bay leaves
sea salt and freshly ground
black pepper

PERI PERI SAUCE

1 large red capsicum (pepper),
roasted, peeled and seeded
1 red bird's eye chilli, roughly
chopped
2 garlic cloves
1 teaspoon ground cumin
1 teaspoon ground coriander
1 teaspoon smoked hot paprika
1 tablespoon lemon juice
1 teaspoon finely grated lemon zest
pinch of sea salt
pinch of sugar
60 ml (2 fl oz/¼ cup) olive oil

METHOD

Preheat the oven to 200°C (400°F/Gas 6).

TO MAKE THE VEGGIES

Lightly oil a large non-stick roasting tray (or line a roasting tray with baking paper).

Quarter the onions, halve the tomatoes lengthways and slice the potatoes into 1.5 cm (⅝ inch) thick slices.

Toss the vegetables, oil, vinegar and herbs together in a large bowl with a pinch of salt and pepper until well coated.

Spread evenly around the tray and roast for 45 minutes, or until the potato is pretty much cooked through. (The fish needs to roast on top of the veggies for the last 15–20 minutes of cooking.)

TO MAKE THE PERI PERI SAUCE

Blitz all of the ingredients, except the olive oil, in a blender until smooth.

Leave the blender running and slowly drizzle in the oil until the mixture is smooth and luscious.

TO PREPARE AND COOK THE FISH

Lightly coat each fish fillet in the peri peri sauce and place on top of the roasting veggies about 15 minutes before they're done cooking.

Roast the fish for 15–20 minutes, or until the fillets are perfectly cooked through and the potato is tender. The cooking time will depend on how thick the fish fillets are.

Scatter the coriander leaves over the fish and veggies, and serve with a leafy green salad.

skirt steak

Serves 8

This isn't something you can wear, it's even better: something you can eat! Skirt steak is a long cut of meat from the 'plate' of the cow, just under the ribs. And although it's a cheaper cut, it has wonderful flavour and can be jazzed up and tenderised so easily with a marinade. It's fantastic for things like tortillas and stir-fries, or even marinated and grilled in one piece on the barbecue. Remember, the longer you marinate the meat the more tender it will be.

TO MAKE THE MARINADE
Blitz all of the ingredients in a food processor until smooth.

TO PREPARE AND COOK THE STEAKS
Combine the steaks and marinade in a shallow dish and turn the meat to coat well. Cover and refrigerate for a few hours, or overnight if possible.
Heat a chargrill pan over high heat until very hot. Lightly brush the pan with olive oil, then add the steaks and cook for 3–4 minutes on each side for medium-rare (which is ideal for this cut of beef).
Rest in a warm spot for 3 minutes.
Thinly slice on the diagonal, across the grain, and serve with a delicious salad.

INGREDIENTS
4 skirt steaks (about 550 g/
    1 lb 4 oz each), well trimmed
olive oil, for brushing

MARINADE
125 ml (4 fl oz/½ cup) white
    wine vinegar
125 ml (4 fl oz/½ cup) olive oil
1 bunch of rosemary, leaves
    stripped and finely chopped
2 tablespoons dijon mustard
1 tablespoon soy sauce
1 teaspoon worcestershire sauce
sea salt and freshly ground
    black pepper
4 garlic cloves

preserved lemon party chickens

Serves 12

If you partially debone the chickens, they will fit snugly in a big roasting tray. They cook beautifully together, releasing delicious, tasty juices, and this leaves space in the oven if you want to roast up some veggies.

INGREDIENTS

3 x 1.6 kg (3 lb 8 oz) chickens (free-range or organic, if you can)

8 garlic cloves

⅓ cup thyme leaves

125 ml (4 fl oz/½ cup) olive oil

2 teaspoons freshly ground white pepper

1 preserved lemon, seeded (I use the skin and flesh)

1 tablespoon smoked hot or sweet paprika

sea salt

METHOD

Preheat the oven to 225°C (440°F/Gas 7½).

Partially debone each chicken. To do this, cut down and along both sides of the spine from the neck to the parson's nose with a pair of kitchen scissors, then remove and discard the spine (or do as I do and save it to make stock).

Flatten each chicken out. If you're feeling handy, use a sharp knife to cut under the ribs and remove them as well.

Blitz the garlic, thyme, olive oil, pepper, preserved lemon and paprika in a food processor to create a paste. Taste and add salt only if it needs it (the preserved lemon is already salty).

Rub the paste all over the chickens. Put them, skin side up, head to tail in a large lightly oiled roasting tray.

Bake for 20 minutes, then reduce the oven temperature to 180°C (350°F/Gas 4) and cook for another 45 minutes, or until cooked through.

Rest the chickens for 10 minutes.

Quarter the chickens then drizzle over their resting juices. I usually serve them with some simple roasted potatoes (or sweet potatoes) and a green salad.

pumpkin, spinach & water chestnut curry

Serves 8

The sweetness of the pumpkin and creaminess of the coconut work beautifully with the aromatics and spices in this Thai-style curry. It's so easy to make your own curry pastes and they taste much better than the store-bought versions. I buy all my curry paste ingredients from my local Asian grocer and usually triple the curry paste recipe to make a big batch. It freezes really well, and I divide it into portions before freezing so it's easy to use when I need it. A curry is always a great way to feed a mob.

INGREDIENTS

1.5 kg (3 lb 5 oz) butternut pumpkin (squash), peeled and cut into 3 cm (1¼ inch) cubes
2 tablespoons peanut oil
sea salt and freshly ground black pepper
3 x 400 ml (14 fl oz) tins coconut milk
4 kaffir lime leaves
1 lemongrass stem, bruised and tied in a knot
1 tablespoon fish sauce (see Note)
squeeze of lime juice
2 teaspoons grated palm sugar (jaggery)
1 x 400 ml (14 fl oz) tin of coconut cream
1 large bunch of coriander (cilantro), leaves and stems only (roots reserved for the green curry paste)
1 x 230 g (8 oz) tin of water chestnuts, drained
360 g (12¾ oz/2 big bunches) English spinach, leaves stripped, washed and chopped
steamed jasmine rice, to serve

GREEN CURRY PASTE

3 red Asian shallots
1 tablespoon finely chopped fresh galangal
1 tablespoon finely chopped fresh ginger
1 tablespoon finely chopped garlic
4 long green chillies
finely grated zest of 1 lemon
10 coriander (cilantro) roots
1 teaspoon shrimp paste (see Note)
½ teaspoon freshly ground white pepper
2 heaped teaspoons ground coriander
1 heaped teaspoon ground cumin
60 ml (2 fl oz/¼ cup) vegetable oil

METHOD

Preheat the oven to 200°C (400°F/Gas 6).

Put the pumpkin in a roasting tray lined with baking paper, drizzle with half of the peanut oil, season with salt and pepper and toss to coat well.

Bake for 20–25 minutes, or until just cooked but still firm.

TO MAKE THE GREEN CURRY PASTE

Blitz all of the ingredients in a blender or food processor until a smooth paste forms.

Heat the remaining tablespoon of peanut oil in a large heavy-based saucepan over medium heat. Add the curry paste and cook for a few minutes until beautifully aromatic. Be careful not to burn the paste.

Add the coconut milk, lime leaves and lemongrass and simmer for about 20 minutes, or until the flavours have infused and the sauce has reduced a little.

Add the fish sauce, lime juice and palm sugar to the curry sauce and taste to check for a nice balance of sweet, sour and salty. Adjust to your liking with extra sugar, lime juice or fish sauce.

Blitz the coconut cream in a blender with the coriander leaves and stems until smooth (reserve a few leaves for garnishing).

Add the coconut cream mixture to the curry sauce along with the roasted pumpkin, water chestnuts and spinach. Gently cook until the spinach has wilted and the pumpkin and water chestnuts have warmed through.

Scatter with the reserved coriander leaves and serve with some jasmine rice.

NOTE If you are feeding vegetarians who prefer not to eat shrimp paste or fish sauce, the best flavour substitute is celery salt and half a vegetable stock cube.

salads

Over the years, salad has been pigeonholed and stereotyped into near extinction by the mixed salad of the '70s and the garden salad of the '80s. Every mum's insistence that you 'Eat your salad!' has not helped. Throw in a bottled dressing from aisle number five, and you can be sure the chooks will get a good feed.

Thankfully, of late there has been a light of hope for our healthy, but marginalised, friend. People have woken up to the endless possibilities that salad brings to their table, and to their diet. Perhaps because salad has been stuck in a rut for so long it has left plenty of room for interpretation. Everything has not been done when it comes to salads, and it won't be for a while yet.

Oh, how I love the blank canvas that is salad! I really get excited by this versatile dish and the amazing variety of seasonal ingredients that we can pull our inspiration from. I love experimenting with the endless combinations of flavours, colours and textures. All the options are too much fun to resist. A beautifully dressed salad really can be the pretty bit on your table; it doesn't have to be the boring sidekick. Make it the headliner.

roasted tomato & chickpea salad

Serves 6–8

This is a gorgeous salad served warm or cold. It can also work well with other pulses and, depending on what I'm serving it with, I sometimes sprinkle some feta cheese over the top.

INGREDIENTS

14 roma (plum) tomatoes, quartered lengthways

4 red onions, cut into 8 wedges each

4 garlic cloves, chopped

2 tablespoons sugar

2 teaspoons sea salt

60 ml (2 fl oz/¼ cup) balsamic vinegar

60 ml (2 fl oz/¼ cup) olive oil

2 x 400 g (14 oz) tins of chickpeas (garbanzo beans), drained and rinsed

1 large bunch coriander (cilantro), leaves picked and roughly chopped

METHOD

Preheat the oven to 140°C (275°F/Gas 1).

Put the tomato, onion and garlic in a large bowl, sprinkle over the sugar and salt, drizzle over the vinegar and oil and toss to combine.

Spread the veggies evenly around a roasting tray and cook for 1½ hours, or until the onion is tender.

If serving warm, gently toss the chickpeas and coriander in a large serving bowl with the vegetables when they come out of the oven.

If serving cold, allow the vegetables to cool before adding the chickpeas and coriander.

deconstructed guacamole

Serves 6–8

I've been making this salad since I was little. You can make it as fine or as chunky as you like, and any leftovers can be mashed up and used as a dip, or spooned over a hot cheese toastie for breakfast. Other ingredients that make great additions to this salad include black beans, chickpeas (garbanzo beans), grilled corn, diced capsicum (pepper) or sunflower sprouts.

METHOD

Combine all of the salad ingredients in a large bowl.
Whisk all of the dressing ingredients together.
Pour the dressing over the salad, gently toss to coat and then serve.

INGREDIENTS

1 large telegraph (long) cucumber, diced
4 large tomatoes, seeded and diced
1 small red onion, finely diced
3 large avocados, destoned and diced
1 cup roughly chopped coriander (cilantro) leaves and stems

DRESSING

60 ml (2 fl oz/¼ cup) freshly squeezed lime juice
60 ml (2 fl oz/¼ cup) extra virgin olive oil
2 garlic cloves, minced
1 teaspoon sea salt
pinch of white sugar
pinch of freshly ground black pepper

upside-down potato salad

Serves 10

I made this salad once on a TV Christmas special and to this day people still stop me in the street to ask for the recipe. The secret is out. Enjoy!

INGREDIENTS

2.2 kg (4 lb 15 oz) potatoes, peeled and cut into 3 cm (1¼ inch) pieces

720 g (1 lb 9½ oz/4 bunches) English spinach, leaves stripped and washed

2 tablespoons butter

2 tablespoons sugar

sea salt and freshly ground black pepper

3 large leeks, white part only, washed and cut into 2 cm (¾ inch) thick rounds

60 ml (2 fl oz/¼ cup) water

2 red capsicums (peppers), roasted, peeled, seeded and thickly sliced

DRESSING

185 g (6½ oz/¾ cup) good-quality mayonnaise

185 g (6½ oz/¾ cup) sour cream

200 g (7 oz/¾ cup) thick Greek-style yoghurt

1 cup finely chopped chives

¼ cup chopped mint

½ cup chopped dill

TO PREPARE THE SALAD

Cook the potato in salted boiling water until just tender, then drain and cool.

Blanch the spinach in a large saucepan of salted boiling water for 30 seconds, or until just wilted.

Drain, then refresh in iced water to stop it cooking further and help preserve its colour.

Drain again, squeeze until dry, then roughly chop.

Melt the butter, sugar and a pinch of salt and pepper in a large frying pan over medium heat until they start to bubble and foam together.

Add the leek and water and gently cook the leek for about 5 minutes on each side, or until tender and caramelised. Allow to cool.

Whisk all of the dressing ingredients together then gently fold the dressing through the cooled potato.

TO ASSEMBLE THE SALAD

Line the base and sides of a 20 cm (8 inch) square cake tin (see Note) with plastic wrap. Decorate the base and sides with some of the spinach, leek rounds and roasted capsicum.

Spoon in one-third of the potato mixture.

Continue layering the remaining ingredients until finished.

Cover with plastic wrap and gently press to compact it. This is best turned out after it has been refrigerated for a few hours to allow it to set properly.

NOTE You can also make this in a large bowl if you want a really impressive dome shape. It can be prepared and refrigerated the day before you eat it.

asian slaw

Serves 6

This famous cabbage salad has had a facelift over the years. I've eaten it dressed up and dressed down, from take-away joints and high-class restaurants. It's celebrated all over the world, and my version sings of hot afternoons and poolside barbecues. It goes particularly well with salty crunchy pork. I've given you a choice of my two favourite dressings, which are both great options.

INGREDIENTS
¼ red cabbage
1 fennel bulb
2 granny smith (green) apples
½ small red onion
150 g (5½ oz) bean sprouts
1 cup coriander (cilantro) leaves
1 cup baby basil leaves
50 g (1¾ oz) thinly sliced pickled
    ginger

DRESSING ONE
2 tablespoons kecap manis
    (see Notes)
2 tablespoons mirin
1 tablespoon rice wine vinegar
2 teaspoons sesame oil

DRESSING TWO
85 g (3 oz/⅓ cup) Kewpie
    (Japanese) mayonnaise
3 tablespoons sour cream
juice of 1 lemon

METHOD
Finely shred the cabbage, fennel, apple and onion using a mandoline if you have one (see Notes).
Mix all of the salad ingredients together in a large bowl.
Whisk all of the dressing ingredients together.
Dress the salad just before serving.

NOTES The tip for success in this recipe is making sure everything is very finely shredded. If you're a keen cook, a mandoline will be one of the best investments you will make in your kitchen, however, a super-sharp vegetable peeler will also do the trick.

Kecap manis is an Indonesian sweet soy sauce sold in good Asian grocers. It can be substituted with soy sauce sweetened with a little brown sugar.

noodle salad

Serves 12

This fresh, vibrant salad ticks every box: it's pretty, colourful, tasty and totally satisfying. I admit, the preparation of the vegetables takes a bit of time, but it's well worth it. You can make this salad with soba, egg or rice noodles.

METHOD

Julienne the carrot, capsicum, spring onion and broccoli stem. Cut the head of the broccoli into small florets.

Cut the squash into small wedges and slice the snow peas on the diagonal.

Bring a large saucepan of lightly salted water to the boil. Blanch the carrot, squash, snow peas and broccoli for 2 minutes, then remove the vegetables with a large slotted spoon and plunge into ice-cold water to stop them cooking further, and to preserve their colour. Drain well.

Bring the water back to boiling point, then cook the noodles according to the packet directions, making sure that they are not overcooked.

Strain the noodles and run under cold water to cool down. Strain well again then toss with the peanut oil to avoid sticking.

Mix the blanched vegetables, noodles and the remaining salad ingredients (except the crispy shallots) gently in a large bowl. I find it easiest to use my hands.

Whisk all of the dressing ingredients together until well combined.

Just before serving, pour the dressing over the salad and scatter over the crispy shallots.

NOTE Crispy shallots are available from the Asian section of most supermarkets or Asian grocers.

INGREDIENTS

1 large carrot
1 large red capsicum (pepper)
4 spring onions (scallions)
1 small head of broccoli
350 g (12 oz) yellow baby squash (pattypan)
250 g (9 oz) snow peas (mangetout), stringed
350 g (12 oz) dried egg noodles
1 tablespoon peanut oil
200 g (7 oz) bean sprouts
1 bunch of coriander (cilantro), leaves and stems only, chopped
$2\frac{1}{2}$ cups basil leaves, thinly sliced
$\frac{1}{2}$ cup mint leaves, thinly sliced
140 g (5 oz/1 cup) unsalted roasted peanuts
crispy shallots, for serving (see Note)

DRESSING

2 teaspoons minced fresh ginger
1 teaspoon minced garlic
1–2 red chillies, finely chopped
1 lemongrass stem, soft inner core only, finely chopped
80 ml ($2\frac{1}{2}$ fl oz/$\frac{1}{3}$ cup) kecap manis (see Notes on page 102)
1 tablespoon sesame oil
1 tablespoon peanut oil
juice of 1 lemon or lime

warm chilli, pumpkin & lentil salad

Serves 4

This salad is great served any time of the year. Eat it warm, straight from the oven in the winter, or serve it cold as a colourful addition to a summery feast.

METHOD

Preheat the oven to 180°C (350°F/Gas 4).

Put the pumpkin, chilli, garlic, ginger, peanut oil and salt and pepper in a large bowl and toss until well coated.

Spread evenly in a non-stick roasting tray (or use a roasting tray lined with baking paper), then roast for 30 minutes, or until the pumpkin is just cooked through but still firm.

Meanwhile, put the lentils and bay leaf in a saucepan with the water and a pinch of salt over medium heat. Cook for 20 minutes, or until soft to the bite, then drain.

Combine the pumpkin and lentils in a large bowl.

Whisk the lemon juice, sugar and salt and pepper for the dressing in a small bowl, then add the onion and set aside until ready to serve. This will soften the sharpness of the onion. When ready to dress the salad, whisk in the oil.

Just before serving, add the coriander to the pumpkin mixture, pour over the dressing and toss together.

NOTE If you want to serve the salad cold, allow all of the ingredients to cool before combining.

INGREDIENTS

1 butternut pumpkin (squash) (about 1 kg/2 lb 4 oz), peeled and roughly cut into 2.5 cm (1 inch) cubes

1 red chilli, finely chopped

1 teaspoon finely chopped garlic

2 teaspoons finely chopped fresh ginger

2 tablespoons peanut oil

sea salt and freshly ground black pepper

210 g ($7\frac{1}{2}$ oz/1 cup) puy (tiny blue-green) lentils, rinsed

1 fresh bay leaf

1 litre (35 fl oz/4 cups) of water

1 cup coriander (cilantro) leaves

DRESSING

juice of 1 lemon

1 teaspoon caster (superfine) sugar

sea salt and freshly ground black pepper

1 small red onion, halved and thinly sliced lengthways

60 ml (2 fl oz/$\frac{1}{4}$ cup) extra virgin olive oil

fennel salad

Serves 4 as a side dish

Fennel is my favourite vegetable at the moment — fresh, aromatic and apparently an aphrodisiac! You wouldn't want to mess with it too much. Keep it simple!

INGREDIENTS

2 large fennel bulbs, tough outer layers and core removed, fronds reserved

2 tablespoons lemon juice

85 g (3 oz/⅓ cup) crème fraîche

100 g (3½ oz/2 cups) sunflower sprouts

sea salt and freshly ground black pepper

METHOD

Use a mandoline or a good vegetable peeler to shave fine slices of fennel into a bowl.

Add the lemon juice immediately and toss to coat well — this not only adds flavour, it also stops the fennel from discolouring.

Mix the crème fraîche into the bowl of shaved fennel.

Lightly fold in the sprouts, tear in the reserved fennel fronds and season with salt and pepper before serving.

quick artichoke & spinach salad

Serves 4–6

I always have a jar of artichokes handy in the pantry. You can jazz them up with a marinade for a quick antipasti platter or throw them over a green salad to make it extra special. This is my answer to a speedy green salad fix.

METHOD

Drain the artichoke hearts and gently squeeze out any excess liquid. Halve each one lengthways.

Combine the garlic, lemon zest and juice, parsley, olive oil and salt and pepper in a bowl. Add the artichokes and allow to marinate until ready to serve.

Put the salad leaves and cucumber in a large bowl and dress with the vinegar and extra virgin olive oil. Top with the artichoke mixture and some shaved parmesan.

INGREDIENTS

400 g (14 oz) jar artichoke hearts
    in brine
2 garlic cloves, minced
finely grated zest of 1 lemon
    and juice of $\frac{1}{2}$ a lemon
1 small bunch of flat-leaf (Italian)
    parsley, leaves roughly
    chopped
60 ml (2 fl oz/$\frac{1}{4}$ cup) olive oil
sea salt and freshly ground
    black pepper
400 g (14 oz) baby spinach leaves
200 g (7 oz) rocket (arugula) leaves
1 telegraph (long) cucumber,
    halved lengthways and
    thinly sliced across
drizzle of raspberry vinegar
drizzle of extra virgin olive oil
shaved parmesan, to serve

quinoa tabouleh

Serves 4

Tabouleh is traditionally made with burghul (bulgur) wheat, but I find it a more texturally interesting salad when made with quinoa. It's a great gluten-free alternative and is super high in protein and iron. Delicious served with fish, chicken or lamb.

INGREDIENTS

300 g (3½ oz/1½ cups) quinoa
  (I use a combination of black,
  red and white)
750 ml (26 fl oz/3 cups) water
sea salt
3 large firm ripe tomatoes,
  quartered, seeded and finely
  diced
½ a large red onion, finely diced
½ a telegraph (long) cucumber,
  finely diced
½ cup roughly chopped mint leaves
1 cup roughly chopped flat-leaf
  (Italian) parsley leaves

DRESSING

3 garlic cloves, finely chopped
125 ml (4 fl oz/½ cup) freshly
  squeezed lemon juice
125 ml (4 fl oz/½ cup) extra virgin
  olive oil
pinch of sugar
sea salt and freshly ground
  black pepper

METHOD

Wash the quinoa in a fine sieve, then strain and put in a medium saucepan with the water and a pinch of salt. Bring to the boil over high heat, then reduce the heat to low–medium and cook for 10 minutes.
Cover with a lid and cook for another 5 minutes on low heat.
Remove from the heat, keep covered and allow to cool.
Whisk all of the dressing ingredients together.
Put the cooled quinoa into a bowl and fluff it up with a fork. Add the remaining ingredients and pour the dressing over the salad.

NOTE In the winter I prefer to serve this salad warm, so I add all of the ingredients and dressing to the quinoa while it's hot.

zucchini, sweet herbs & persian feta cheese

Serves 4 as a side dish

We don't often eat zucchini raw, but it has a wonderful texture if you slice it thinly and marinate it in a citrus dressing. This is a simple fresh, zingy side salad I like to serve with lamb or fish. I think dill and marjoram go beautifully with zucchini but you can use any of your favourite soft herbs; basil and mint can also be great additions, especially if you're serving it with lamb.

METHOD

Thinly slice the zucchini lengthways. I use a mandoline, but you can also use a good sharp vegetable peeler to get the same result. Put the slices in a large wide-based dish and sprinkle lightly with salt, pepper and the lemon zest.

Lightly whisk the lemon juice, extra virgin olive oil, sugar and garlic together to make a dressing.

Drizzle the dressing all over the zucchini.

Cover and allow to marinate for about 20 minutes, then transfer the marinated zucchini to a serving platter, reserving any marinade from the dish to pour over at the end.

Crumble the feta over the zucchini and scatter over the herbs. Drizzle over the reserved marinade and serve.

NOTE Make sure you only grate the yellow zest of the lemon and not the white pith, as it can be bitter.

INGREDIENTS

2 zucchini (courgettes)

sea salt and freshly ground
    black pepper

finely grated zest and juice
    of 1 lemon (see Note)

125 ml (4 fl oz/½ cup) extra virgin
    olive oil

pinch of white sugar

1 small garlic clove, minced

80 g (2¾ oz) Persian feta cheese,
    crumbled

1 tablespoon roughly chopped
    marjoram

2 tablespoons roughly chopped
    dill

dukkah-spiced eggplant with goat's curd & yoghurt dressing

Serves 4

Dukkah is a roasted Egyptian spice mix laced with seeds and nuts. It's easy to make if you have the time and ingredients handy, but there are also lots of great blends available at local farmers' markets or gourmet food shops. Simple wedges of roasted eggplant are transformed into a super side dish at any table when they're encrusted in this aromatic spice mix.

EGGPLANT
80 ml (2½ fl oz/⅓ cup) olive oil
2 garlic cloves, minced
sea salt and freshly ground
    black pepper
2 eggplants (aubergines),
    cut into 8 wedges each
50 g (1¾ oz) dukkah spice mix

DRESSING
130 g (4½ oz/½ cup) thick
    Greek-style yoghurt
70 g (2½ oz) goat's curd
squeeze of lemon, to taste
pinch of salt
pinch of white pepper
pinch of sugar

TO SERVE
pomegranate molasses,
    for drizzling
coriander (cilantro) leaves, to
    garnish
toasted sesame seeds (optional),
    to garnish

METHOD
Preheat the oven to 200°C (400°F/Gas 6).
Combine the olive oil and garlic for the eggplant in a small bowl and season with salt and pepper.
Arrange the eggplant wedges on a baking tray lined with baking paper. Lightly brush the wedges with the seasoned oil.
Roast for 20 minutes, or until the eggplant wedges are lightly golden and tender to the touch, but still holding their shape.
Remove from the oven and, while they're still warm, coat each side of the eggplant wedges with the dukkah.
Whisk all of the dressing ingredients together in a bowl until smooth.
Arrange the eggplant wedges on a long platter and spoon over the dressing. Lightly drizzle with the pomegranate molasses, and scatter over the coriander and sesame seeds (if using).

baby beets with broad beans & labneh

Serves 4–6

Labneh is yoghurt that has been strained in a cloth (traditionally made of muslin), to remove the whey. This process gives it a soft cheese-like texture, while preserving the yoghurt's distinctive tang. The earthiness of the beetroot and beans paired with the creamy tang of the labneh make a gorgeous combination.

METHOD

Strain the yoghurt in the fridge overnight in a fine sieve or muslin (cheesecloth) placed over a bowl to catch the whey.

The next day, trim the leaves and stems off the beetroot, leaving 2.5 cm (1 inch) of the stem intact.

Steam the beetroot in their skins for about 20 minutes, or until they can be easily pierced with a fork.

Remove the skins and stems under cold running water with your fingers (wear rubber gloves if you don't want pink hands). If the beetroot are perfectly cooked, the skins should slide off easily.

Cook the broad beans in boiling water for 3–4 minutes (or 1 minute if using frozen beans), then drain and run under cold water to stop them cooking further.

Pinch each bean between your fingers to remove the skin then put the beans in a small bowl, drizzle over some olive oil, squeeze over some of the lemon juice and season with salt and pepper.

Halve the beetroot and put in a bowl, drizzle over some olive oil and lemon juice and season with salt and pepper.

Spoon the beetroot and beans over your favourite platter then top with quenelles (pretty little spoonfuls) of labneh. Scatter over the chives or mint leaves (or both), drizzle with some more olive oil then serve.

INGREDIENTS

300 g (10½ oz) thick Greek-style yoghurt

1 kg (2 lb 4 oz) baby beetroot (beets)

400 g (14 oz) podded broad (fava) beans

drizzle of extra virgin olive oil

½ a lemon

sea salt and freshly ground black pepper

a few chives or mint leaves, sliced, to garnish

what's for dinner, mum?

I grew up in a family of six in the '70s ... or should I say 'the brown food days'? Mum fed us to fill us up, not because she had some great urge to get into the kitchen and unleash her inner gourmet goddess. She burnt toast on a regular basis and burnt her bra for women's liberation. Once we were all in school, she became a full-time working mum. We would often get home before her, and as soon as she walked in the door she'd ask us how our day at school was, and we would reply, 'What's for dinner, Mum?'

So I dedicate this chapter to all the mums (and dads) out there who scramble for ideas when asked this question. And, of course, to my mum, who more than made up for her lack of creativity in the kitchen with her intelligence, warmth and wit.

nacho bake

Serves 6–8

I just know this will be the recipe my kids take with them when they leave home. It's a great informal Friday-night feed. You can double up on the amount of beans and leave out the meat to make this a vegetarian dish. If your kids don't like spices, you can also leave out the chilli, paprika and cayenne pepper.

INGREDIENTS

2 tablespoons olive oil
2 brown onions, finely diced
3 garlic cloves, minced
1 kg (2 lb 4 oz) minced (ground) beef
2 teaspoons smoked hot paprika
3 teaspoons ground cumin
1 teaspoon chilli flakes
1 teaspoon cayenne pepper
    (optional)
2 teaspoons ground coriander
1 teaspoon dried oregano
3 x 400 g (14 oz) tins of chopped
    tomatoes
3 x 400 g (14 oz) tins of kidney
    beans, drained and rinsed
sea salt and freshly ground
    black pepper
500 g (1 lb 2 oz) natural corn chips
125 g (4½ oz/1¼ cups) grated
    cheddar cheese

TO SERVE

sour cream
3 avocados, destoned, smashed
    and seasoned with a squeeze
    of lime juice
a handful of fresh coriander
    (cilantro) leaves, to garnish

METHOD

Preheat the oven to 180°C (350°F/Gas 4).
Heat the olive oil in a large heavy-based saucepan over medium heat. Add the onion and garlic and cook for 5–6 minutes, or until the onion is translucent.
Add the beef and spices and cook, breaking up the meat with the back of a wooden spoon, for 10 minutes, or until the meat is lightly browned.
Stir in the tomatoes and beans and season with salt and pepper.
Reduce the heat to low and simmer for 20 minutes, or until the mixture reaches a thick sauce consistency.
Pour the sauce into a shallow 3.5 litre (122 fl oz/ 14 cup) capacity baking dish, cover with the corn chips and scatter over the cheese.
Bake for 15 minutes, or until the cheese is melted and golden.
Serve with sour cream, smashed avocado dip and some coriander leaves scattered on top.

chicken pan pie

Serves 6–8

I love pies. As a teenager, whenever I discovered a good one it would make my daily diary. The classic combination of chicken and leek is one of my favourites and the addition of creamy mushrooms, spinach and fennel takes it to another level. Any leftovers (if you're lucky) taste great reheated the next day.

INGREDIENTS

1 kg (2 lb 4 oz) skinless, boneless chicken thigh fillets (free-range or organic, if you can), excess fat trimmed

sea salt and freshly ground black pepper

3 teaspoons fennel seeds

2 tablespoons olive oil, plus extra for greasing

1 leek, white part only, halved lengthways and thinly sliced

3 garlic cloves, minced

100 g (3½ oz) speck or bacon, thinly sliced

350 g (12 oz) button mushrooms, sliced

250 ml (9 fl oz/1 cup) dry white wine

375 ml (13 fl oz/1½ cups) good-quality chicken stock

2 tablespoons cornflour (cornstarch)

180 g (6½ oz/1 bunch) English spinach, leaves blanched, squeezed dry and chopped

4 sheets puff pastry

1 egg yolk, lightly beaten

METHOD

Preheat the oven to 200°C (400°F/Gas 6).

Put the chicken in a roasting tray, sprinkle with some salt, pepper and the fennel seeds, cover with foil and bake for 25 minutes, or until cooked through.

Remove the chicken from the oven and, when cool enough to touch, chop into chunky pieces and reserve any juices.

Reduce the oven temperature to 190°C (375°F/Gas 5).

Heat the olive oil in a wide heavy-based saucepan over medium heat. Add the leek, garlic and speck and cook for a few minutes, or until the leek has softened.

Add the mushroom and cook for a few minutes.

Add the wine to deglaze the pan, then add the stock and any reserved juices from the chicken. Simmer over low heat to reduce a little.

Mix the cornflour with 2 tablespoons of water in a small bowl until smooth, then pour into the pan while stirring continuously with a wooden spoon to avoid lumps forming. The sauce will thicken slightly.

Add the chicken and spinach to the pan and stir to coat in the sauce. Taste for seasoning. Remove from the heat and cool.

Lightly grease a 30 cm (12 inch) non-stick ovenproof frying pan. Join two sheets of pastry together to make one large sheet that will cover the base and sides of the pan, leaving the pastry overhanging a little and cutting it to fit where necessary.

Spoon the cooled filling into the pastry-lined pan.

Join the two remaining sheets of pastry together to make one large square, and cover the pie, pinching the edges together to seal them. Decorate as you like.

Prick the lid with a fork and brush with the beaten egg yolk to give it a nice glaze.

Bake for 25–30 minutes, or until golden (see Note).

NOTE I bake my pie in the middle shelf of the oven for the first 15–20 minutes and when it's slightly golden and puffed up, I transfer it to the lowest shelf or the actual bottom of the oven for the last 10 minutes to ensure a crispy base.

lollipop chops with roasted veg couscous

Serves 6

Feeding kids often involves clever marketing. Just mention lollipop chops in our house and the kids start asking 'When's dinner ready?' every five minutes!

LOLLIPOP CHOPS

60 ml (2 fl oz/¼ cup) olive oil

1 bunch of thyme, leaves stripped

finely grated zest of 1 lemon

4 garlic cloves, minced

sea salt and freshly ground black pepper

18 lamb cutlets, French trimmed

ROASTED VEG COUSCOUS

2 red onions, cut into 8 wedges each

2 red capsicums (peppers), cut into
   2.5 cm (1 inch) pieces

1 large zucchini (courgette), cut into
   2.5 cm (1 inch) pieces

350 g (12 oz) sweet potatoes, peeled
   and cut into 2.5 cm (1 inch) pieces

2 tablespoons olive oil, plus extra
   for drizzling

sea salt and freshly ground black pepper

380 g (13½ oz/2 cups) couscous

500 ml (17 fl oz/2 cups) boiling water
   or hot vegetable stock

95 g (3¼ oz/1 cup) flaked almonds, toasted

2 tablespoons chopped preserved lemon
   (I use the skin and flesh) (see Note)

1 bunch of mint, leaves sliced

1 bunch of coriander (cilantro), leaves and
   stems roughly chopped

1 bunch of flat-leaf (Italian) parsley, leaves
   roughly chopped

TO MAKE THE ROAST VEG COUSCOUS

Preheat the oven to 180°C (350°F/Gas 4).

Toss the onion, capsicum, zucchini and sweet potato together in a large bowl with the olive oil and a good pinch of salt and pepper until well coated.

Spread the veggies evenly around a large non-stick roasting tray (or a roasting tray lined with baking paper) and cook for 45 minutes, or until the veg are just tender.

Put the couscous and a drizzle of olive oil in a large bowl, pour over the water or stock, cover with plastic wrap and allow to sit for 5 minutes to absorb the liquid. Fluff up the couscous with a fork.

Fold the roasted veg, flaked almonds, preserved lemon and herbs into the couscous, and then taste for seasoning.

TO MAKE THE LOLLIPOP CHOPS

Combine the olive oil, thyme, lemon zest and garlic in a large bowl, and season with salt and pepper. Add the lamb cutlets and toss to coat well.

Preheat the barbecue or a chargrill pan to high. Cook the lamb for about 2 minutes on each side to get a nice juicy pink cutlet, or cook a little longer to your liking.

Rest the lamb for 2 minutes.

Serve the lamb with the roasted veg couscous and minted yoghurt (see page 70).

NOTE If you don't have any preserved lemons for the couscous, you can add some fresh lemon zest (the yellow zest, not the bitter white pith), a squeeze of lemon juice and a pinch of salt to give the couscous a bright lift.

creamy coconut fish curry

Serves 6

This is a gentle introduction to the aromas and flavours of curry, so it's a great one for kids and adults to enjoy together. The addition of sour cream and desiccated coconut softens the spices and sweetens the fish. My girlfriend, Nancy, made this for me once; I watched her kids devour it and I was sold.

TO COOK THE FISH

Preheat the oven to 180°C (350°F/Gas 4).

Lightly grease a roasting tray (preferably non-stick) and generously grease a sheet of baking paper with the butter.

Put the fish in the greased tray, pour over the wine and cover with the baking paper, greased side down.

Bake for about 10 minutes, or until almost cooked through (the exact time will depend on the thickness of the fillets), then remove from the oven and set aside, keeping any cooking juices.

TO MAKE THE CURRY

Melt the butter in a large frying pan over low heat. Add the leek and cook for 4–5 minutes, or until translucent.

Add the garlic, ginger and spices and cook for 2 minutes.

Add the tomato paste, chilli and lemon juice, then cover and cook over very low heat for about 5 minutes.

Add the coconut, sour cream, sugar, water and any cooking juices from the fish to the pan, then simmer for about 10 minutes.

Gently put the fish into the pan and coat with the sauce to reheat.

Turn off the heat, divide the fish and the sauce between your serving bowls. Top each portion with some cucumber ribbons and coriander then serve.

FISH

50 g (1¾ oz) butter, for greasing

1 kg (2 lb 4 oz) firm white fish fillets (such as snapper)

250 ml (9 fl oz/1 cup) dry white wine

cucumber ribbons, to garnish

handful of coriander (cilantro) leaves, to garnish

CURRY SAUCE

130 g (4½ oz) butter

1 leek, white part only, thinly sliced

2 garlic cloves, finely chopped

2 teaspoons grated fresh ginger

3 teaspoons ground coriander

3 teaspoons ground cumin

2 teaspoons ground turmeric

2 teaspoons sweet paprika

1 tablespoon tomato paste (concentrated purée)

2 teaspoons finely chopped red chilli, or to taste

squeeze of lemon juice

45 g (1½ oz/½ cup) desiccated coconut

245 g (8½ oz/1 cup) sour cream

2 teaspoons sugar

185 ml (6 fl oz/¾ cup) water

smoked salmon fusilli

Serves 4

This posh pasta is made with smoked salmon, capers, dill and a touch of cream — all the lovely stuff. It's a very quick recipe to make and it also works well with tinned tuna if you don't have any salmon.

INGREDIENTS

500 g (1 lb 2 oz) fusilli
drizzle of olive oil
½ a red onion, finely diced
3 garlic cloves, minced
juice of 1 lemon
300 ml (10½ fl oz) thin
    (pouring) cream
1 bunch of broccolini, broken into
    florets, stems thinly sliced
220 g (7¾ oz) smoked salmon,
    thinly sliced
60 g (2¼ oz/⅓ cup) tiny capers,
    rinsed
1 bunch of dill, finely chopped
1 bunch of chives, finely chopped
finely grated zest of 1 lemon
pinch of freshly grated nutmeg
sea salt and freshly ground
    black pepper

METHOD

Cook the pasta in a large saucepan of salted boiling water until *al dente*.

Meanwhile, heat the olive oil in a large heavy-based frying pan over low heat. Add the onion and garlic and cook for 5 minutes, or until the onion has softened.

Add the lemon juice to deglaze the pan, then add the cream and simmer for 5 minutes, or until the sauce thickens a little.

Add the broccolini to the pasta water for the last minute of cooking.

Drain the pasta and broccolini together, then return to the pan and drizzle with a little olive oil to stop the pasta from sticking.

Add the sauce to the pasta and broccolini, and gently toss to coat.

Stir in the salmon, capers, dill, chives, lemon zest and nutmeg, and season with salt and pepper.

Dinner's ready, 'Come and get it!'

chicken lovely legs puttanesca on risoni

Serves 4–6

There was nothing I loved more than watching my young babies' faces as I introduced them to new tastes and textures. Scoffed down or spat out, the response was pretty clear! Encourage your kids to experiment with food from a young age and you may just expand their taste buds. This family favourite gently introduces them to robust ingredients and flavours with gusto.

METHOD

Preheat the oven to 180°C (350°F/Gas 4).

Heat half of the olive oil in a large flameproof casserole dish over low–medium heat.

Finely dice the onion, thinly slice the leek and add to the pan with the garlic, sage leaves, rosemary and oregano and cook for 5–6 minutes, or until the onion and leek have softened.

Rinse the capers, pit and halve the olives and finely chop the chilli (if using). Add those ingredients to the pan with the tomatoes, water, anchovies and bay leaves then simmer over low heat for about 10 minutes, or until slightly thickened.

Meanwhile, generously coat the chicken drumsticks in flour and heat the remaining olive oil in a large frying pan over medium heat.

Add the chicken and cook until golden all over, then transfer to the sauce.

Deglaze the frying pan with the wine, then tip the pan juices into the casserole dish and cover.

Bake for 40 minutes, or until the chicken is tender.

Stir through the parsley and season with salt and pepper before serving.

Cook the risoni according to packet directions.

Serve the chicken with the risoni.

INGREDIENTS

125 ml (4 fl oz/½ cup) olive oil

1 brown onion

1 leek, white part only

5 garlic cloves, finely chopped

5 sage leaves

1 tablespoon chopped rosemary

1 tablespoon chopped oregano

50 g (1¾ oz/¼ cup) tiny capers

95 g (3¼ oz/½ cup) kalamata olives

1 small red chilli (optional)

4 x 400 g (14 oz) tins of chopped tomatoes

125 ml (4 fl oz/½ cup) of water

8 anchovy fillets, thinly sliced

2 fresh bay leaves

12 plump chicken drumsticks (free-range or organic, if you can), ends removed

75 g (2½ oz/½ cup) plain (all-purpose) flour

250 ml (9 fl oz/1 cup) dry white wine

1 cup flat-leaf (Italian) parsley leaves

sea salt and freshly ground black pepper

500 g (1 lb 2 oz) risoni (orzo)

mum's lamb stew

Serves 6–8

As comforting as your doona on a winter's morning, whenever I make a stew I feel right at home. This is Mum's version dolled up with some fresh herbs and a splash of red wine.

LAMB STEW

splash of olive oil
2 brown onions, roughly chopped
5 large garlic cloves, finely chopped
4–5 celery stalks, roughly chopped
2 large carrots, roughly chopped
2 potatoes, roughly chopped
1 small sweet potato, roughly
    chopped (optional)
1.5 kg (3 lb 5 oz) braising
    lamb, diced
150 g (5½ oz/1 cup) plain
    (all-purpose) flour
250 ml (9 fl oz/1 cup) red wine
500 ml (17 fl oz/2 cups) water
1 tablespoon tomato paste
    (concentrated purée)
3 tomatoes, roughly chopped
2 tablespoons rosemary leaves,
    chopped
sea salt and freshly ground
    black pepper

GREMOLATA

1 cup flat-leaf (Italian) parsley
    leaves, finely chopped
2 large garlic cloves, finely grated
finely grated zest of 1 lemon
½ teaspoon sea salt

TO MAKE THE STEW

Preheat the oven to 170°C (325°F/Gas 3).

Heat the olive oil in a large frying pan over medium heat. Add the onion and garlic and cook for a few minutes, or until the onion has softened.

Add the celery, carrot, potato and sweet potato (if using), and cook, stirring occasionally, for about 5 minutes. Transfer to a heavy-based flameproof casserole dish.

Heat another splash of olive oil in the frying pan. Put half the lamb and half the flour in a plastic bag and shake to coat well. Shake off the excess flour, then add the lamb to the pan and cook until lightly browned all over.

Deglaze the pan with a little of the wine, then transfer the lamb to the casserole dish.

Add a little more oil to the pan and repeat with the remaining meat, flour and wine.

Add the water, tomato paste, tomato and rosemary to the casserole dish, season with salt and pepper, and cover with a tight-fitting lid.

Bake for 2 hours, or until the lamb is tender (see Note).

TO MAKE THE GREMOLATA

Wrap the parsley in muslin (cheesecloth) or a clean tea towel and squeeze out and discard the juice.

Toss the parsley, garlic, lemon zest and salt together in a small bowl, then scatter over the lamb stew.

NOTE Alternatively, you can cook the stew on the stovetop over very low heat. My mum used to cook hers in a pressure cooker.

semolina gnocchi with blue castello & spinach sauce

Serves 4

I love a good gnocchi. Making potato gnocchi has always been a labour of love for me, so whipping up quick semolina gnocchi somehow makes me feel like I'm cheating. But this Roman-style gnocchi is so easy to prepare and is a total triumph with the kids. You can bake or fry it, and serve it with a roasted tomato sauce or something creamy — my kids love it with a creamy sauce, so here's the recipe.

SEMOLINA GNOCCHI
2 tablespoons butter, plus extra
    for greasing and cooking
750 ml (26 fl oz/3 cups) milk
10 gratings of nutmeg
1 thyme sprig
1 fresh bay leaf
1 teaspoon sea salt
freshly ground black pepper
180 g (6¼ oz/1 cup) fine semolina
50 g (1¾ oz/½ cup) grated pecorino cheese
1 egg, lightly beaten

BLUE CASTELLO SAUCE
30 g (1 oz) butter
1 small brown onion, finely diced
2 garlic cloves, minced
100 ml (3½ fl oz) dry white wine or
    good-quality chicken stock
300 ml (10½ fl oz) thin (pouring) cream
150 g (5½ oz) blue castello cheese or other
    creamy blue cheese, chopped
180 g (6½ oz/1 bunch) English spinach,
    leaves stripped, washed and shredded
sea salt and freshly ground black pepper

TO SERVE
shaved parmesan cheese, to garnish
toasted pine nuts, to garnish

TO MAKE THE SEMOLINA GNOCCHI

Lightly grease and line the base and sides of a 22 cm (8½ inch) square cake tin with baking paper.

Put the milk, nutmeg, thyme, bay leaf, salt, pepper and butter in a large heavy-based saucepan over medium heat and simmer for a few minutes to allow the butter to melt and flavours to infuse. Remove the bay leaf and thyme.

Whisking continuously, gradually add the semolina to the pan and combine well.

Reduce the heat to low and cook for 3–4 minutes, stirring vigorously with a wooden spoon until the mixture thickens and starts to pull away from the side of the pan.

Remove from the heat and stir in the pecorino and beaten egg.

Spoon the dough into the prepared tin, and spread evenly so that it is about 2 cm (¾ inch) thick. I use my hands for this, and lightly oil them to avoid sticking.

Chill the dough in the fridge for about 30 minutes to set.

Cut the dough into 4–5 cm (1½–2 inch) rounds or squares. Re-roll any off-cuts and use them.

TO MAKE THE BLUE CASTELLO SAUCE

Melt the butter in a medium heavy-based frying pan over low–medium heat. Add the onion and garlic and cook for 5–6 minutes, or until the onion has softened.

Add the wine or stock and simmer until reduced by half.

Add the cream and continue to reduce until the sauce reaches a coating consistency.

Add the blue cheese and spinach, season with salt and pepper, and stir until the spinach has wilted.

TO SERVE

Pan-fry the gnocchi, in batches, in a generous amount of melted butter until crispy and lightly browned on both sides.

Pour the hot castello sauce over the gnocchi.

Garnish with the parmesan and pine nuts and serve with a simple salad and crusty bread.

NOTE If you prefer, you can bake the gnocchi rather than fry it. Arrange them in a greased casserole dish so that they are just overlapping, brush them lightly with melted butter, then sprinkle with extra parmesan and bake in an oven preheated to 200°C (400°F/Gas 6) for 15–20 minutes, or until golden and crispy. Serve with the hot cheese sauce poured over.

beef burritos with green sauce & salsa

Serves 4

My kids are teenagers now and — like lots of other kids and teenagers — they love a good Mexican feed. I always make my own spice mix, sauce and salsa, not just because I'm a food maniac, but also because I like all my food preservative free. When it's made fresh, at home, it just tastes better.

MEXICAN SPICED STEAK

1 teaspoon dried oregano

1 teaspoon chilli flakes

1 teaspoon cumin seeds, ground

½ teaspoon smoked sweet paprika

½ teaspoon sea salt

freshly ground black pepper

2 x 400 g (14 oz) rump steaks

vegetable oil, for brushing

GREEN SAUCE

1 large bunch of coriander (cilantro), leaves
    and stems only

1 large garlic clove

1 teaspoon soft brown sugar

1 long green chilli, roughly chopped

½ teaspoon sea salt

60 ml (2 fl oz/¼ cup) lime or lemon juice

2 tablespoons vegetable oil

SIMPLE SALSA

2 avocados, destoned and diced

½ a small red onion, finely diced

2 tomatoes, diced

juice of 1 lime or ½ a lemon

drizzle of vegetable oil

sea salt and freshly ground
    black pepper

TO SERVE

4 tortillas

sour cream

shredded lettuce

grated cheddar cheese

TO MAKE THE MEXICAN SPICED STEAK

Mix all of the spices together and rub over the steaks.

Heat a heavy-based frying pan over high heat, lightly brush the steaks with oil and cook for 4 minutes on each side for medium-rare. Rest for 5 minutes before slicing thinly.

TO MAKE THE GREEN SAUCE

Blitz all of the ingredients in a food processor until smooth.

Taste for a balance of citrus, sugar and salt and adjust according to your taste.

TO MAKE THE SIMPLE SALSA

Combine all of the ingredients and season with salt and pepper.

TO SERVE

Put the tortillas, sliced steak, green sauce and salsa (and sour cream, lettuce and cheese if you like) on the table so everyone can assemble their own burritos.

coconut-crusted whiting

Serves 4

Whiting found off the coast of Western Australia is one of our most sustainable fish. I'm a huge fan of the king george and small sand whiting because they have a particularly delicate, sweet flavour that kids seem to love. Once pan-fried, with a crunchy coconut exterior, who can resist — young or old?

METHOD

Put the flour, salt and white pepper on a large plate and stir to evenly distribute.

Put the coconut on a separate plate.

Whisk the eggs and milk in a bowl using a fork.

Dust the whiting fillets, a few at a time, in the seasoned flour until well coated. Shake off any excess flour.

Dip into the egg mixture, coat well then allow the excess to drain off.

Coat the fish generously in the coconut, patting it on with your hands to ensure it sticks all over.

Put the coated fillets on a tray lined with baking paper, and refrigerate for about 30 minutes to help the coconutty crust set.

Heat a large knob of butter and a good splash of olive oil together in a large non-stick frying pan over medium heat. Add the coated fillets and cook for a few minutes on each side until golden and cooked through.

Drain on paper towel. (If you do this in two batches, pop the cooked fish in a preheated hot oven for a minute to keep warm while you fry the second batch. You may need to add some more oil and butter to the pan, for frying.)

Serve the fillets with some lemon or lime wedges for squeezing over and your kids' favourite vegetables — either steamed or in a simple salad.

NOTE You can use any firm white-fleshed fish for this, but if you are using a larger piece of fish, I recommend slicing it into 3 cm (1¼ inch) batons to maximise the coconutty crunch.

INGREDIENTS

150 g (5½ oz/1 cup) plain (all-purpose) flour

pinch of sea salt and freshly ground white pepper

200 g (7 oz) shredded coconut

2 eggs

125 ml (4 fl oz/½ cup) milk

500 g (1 lb 2 oz) small sand whiting fillets, skinned and pinboned (see Note)

butter, for frying

olive oil, for frying

lemon or lime wedges, for serving

herby lemon chicken thighs

Serves 4

I always buy free-range and organic chooks when I can because they taste so good, and because my teenagers already have enough hormones floating around in their bodies. I'm a big fan of chicken thighs because they are so moist, and even if you overcook them to get them crispier they still manage to maintain their tenderness. This recipe sums up everything I love about eating chicken with crispy, delicious skin.

INGREDIENTS

1 heaped tablespoon finely
    chopped thyme leaves
1 heaped tablespoon finely
    chopped rosemary leaves
1 heaped tablespoon finely
    chopped sweet marjoram
    or oregano leaves
6 garlic cloves, minced
finely grated zest and juice
    of 1 lemon
60 ml (2 fl oz/¼ cup) olive oil
1 teaspoon sea salt
8 chicken thighs (free-range
    or organic, if you can), skin
    on and bone in

METHOD

Preheat the oven to 190°C (375°F/Gas 5).
Mix the herbs together in a large bowl with the garlic, lemon zest and juice, olive oil and salt.
Add the chicken and toss to coat well.
Put the chicken, skin side up, on a wire rack placed over a roasting tray.
Roast for about 30–40 minutes, or until crispy and cooked through.
Serve the chicken with steamed vegetables or a salad. This goes really well with the quinoa tabouleh on page 110.

whole-chicken & corn soup

Serves 6

I add chicken necks to this soup because they give the dish more flavour, but if you don't have any you can also add an extra flavour boost with a cheeky stock cube (one that doesn't contain any nasty additives).

METHOD

Heat the olive oil in a large heavy-based flameproof casserole (or a saucepan big enough to hold the whole chicken) over low–medium heat. Add the onion and garlic and cook for 5 minutes, or until the onion has softened.

Add the leek, carrot and celery and cook for 5 minutes.

Add the whole chicken, chicken necks, water, bay leaves, bouquet garni, celery salt and peppercorns, then bring to the boil.

Reduce the heat to low and simmer for 1½ hours, regularly skimming away any foam that rises to the top.

Carefully lift the whole chicken out of the stock and put it in a large bowl to cool a little.

Scoop out and discard the chicken necks, bay leaves and the bouquet garni. Blitz the cooked vegetables and stock together using a hand-held blender.

Remove the chicken meat from the bones. Break it up into chunks and put it back into the soup.

Add the creamed corn and kernels and the parsley and gently reheat. Taste and season if needed.

Serve with warm crusty bread.

NOTE It's a good idea to blanch the chicken in a separate saucepan of boiling water for 1 minute to remove any impurities before you add it to the rest of the ingredients. You won't have to scoop as much scum off the top of the stock as it cooks, and you also won't lose as many of the floating herbs.

INGREDIENTS

2 tablespoons olive oil

1 brown onion, diced

5 garlic cloves, sliced

1 leek, white part only, sliced

3 carrots, cut into rounds

4 celery stalks, roughly chopped

1 whole chook (chicken) (free-range or organic, if you can) (about 1.5 kg/3 lb 5 oz) (see Note)

10 chicken necks (free-range or organic, if you can)

2.5 litres (87 fl oz/10 cups) cold water

2 fresh bay leaves

1 tablespoon dried bouquet garni (mixed herbs) or 1 fresh bouquet garni wrapped in muslin (cheesecloth)

1 teaspoon celery salt

6–8 whole black peppercorns

3 x 400 g (14 oz) tins of creamed corn

2 cups corn kernels (frozen, tinned or fresh)

1 cup flat-leaf (Italian) parsley leaves, chopped

6 slices of bread or warm crusty rolls, to serve

quick beef & broccolini stir-fry

Serves 4

Everyone has their own version of a stir-fry, and mine varies depending on what's left in the fridge. I usually start by frying the aromatics with thinly sliced meat, then I throw in the veg and flavour it up with something sweet, sour and salty. This recipe also works well with rice.

INGREDIENTS

60 ml (2 fl oz/¼ cup) peanut oil

400 g (14 oz) beef rump, very thinly sliced

3 large garlic cloves, finely chopped

1 lemongrass stem, pale part only, thinly sliced

1 tablespoon finely chopped fresh ginger

1 red chilli, seeded and finely chopped

1 large red capsicum (pepper), seeded and sliced

1 bunch of broccolini, halved, stems separated from florets

175 g (6 oz/1½ cups) bean sprouts, trimmed

1 tablespoon fish sauce

1 tablespoon soy sauce

1 tablespoon kecap manis (see Notes)

280 g (10 oz) dried egg noodles, cooked and drained

2 limes

crispy shallots, to serve (see Notes)

small handful of coriander (cilantro) leaves, to serve

small handful of basil leaves, to serve

METHOD

Heat the peanut oil in a large wok over high heat. Add the beef, garlic, lemongrass, ginger and chilli, and stir-fry for about 2 minutes.

Add the capsicum, broccolini florets and stems and cook for 3 minutes.

Add the bean sprouts, fish sauce, soy sauce, kecap manis, cooked noodles and the juice of 1 lime, then toss and cook everything together for 1 minute.

Serve right away, with some crispy shallots and herbs scattered on top, and wedges of lime for squeezing over.

NOTES Kecap manis is an Indonesian sweet soy sauce. It's available from good Asian grocers, and can be substituted with soy sauce sweetened with a little brown sugar.

Crispy shallots are available from the Asian section in most supermarkets or Asian grocers.

pork bolognese

Serves 6–8

Spaghetti bolognese — we all grew up on it and everyone's family recipe tasted different. I've been changing it up lately to a pork bolognese, and the secret to my version is using a good-quality mince and adding a small amount of veal or beef to give it more depth of flavour. I don't use tomatoes in this recipe, just the concentrated purée. The addition of spices, cream, stock and wine give this bolognese a pleasurable light and silky finish.

METHOD

Heat the olive oil in your largest heavy-based saucepan over medium heat. Add the onion and cook for 3–4 minutes, or until translucent, being careful it doesn't burn.

Add the garlic, rosemary and fennel seeds and cook for 1 minute, or until the garlic has lightly browned.

Add the carrot and celery and cook for 3 minutes.

Add the pork and veal, breaking the meat apart with a wooden spoon, to keep it from clumping together. Cook for 5 minutes, or until the meat is cooked and the moisture has evaporated.

Add the wine to deglaze the pan and continue to cook until the liquid has reduced by half.

Add the stock, tomato paste, cinnamon stick, bay leaves and nutmeg, and season with the salt and a pinch or two of pepper.

Reduce the heat to low and simmer for 30 minutes, or until thick and reduced.

Stir in the cream at the end and cook for a few minutes, or until just heated through.

Serve spooned over your favourite spaghetti with a few sliced flat-leaf (Italian) parsley leaves scattered on top.

INGREDIENTS

2 tablespoons olive oil

2 large brown onions, finely chopped

5 garlic cloves, finely chopped

2 tablespoons finely chopped rosemary leaves

2 tablespoons fennel seeds

1 large carrot, finely chopped

3 celery stalks, finely chopped

850 g (1 lb 14 oz) minced (ground) pork

400 g (14 oz) minced (ground) veal

250 ml (9 fl oz/1 cup) dry white wine

500 ml (17 fl oz/2 cups) good-quality veal stock (or beef or chicken stock)

140 g (5 oz) tomato paste (concentrated purée)

1 cinnamon stick

2 fresh bay leaves

10 gratings of nutmeg

1 teaspoon sea salt

freshly ground black pepper

250 ml (9 fl oz/1 cup) thin (pouring) cream

cooked spaghetti, to serve

sticky chicken wings with oriental risotto

Serves 4

Chicken wings are the yummiest and most affordable way to feed a big family. I'm yet to meet an adult or kid who doesn't love and adore these. The chicken wings alone are great to serve at a party, and if you have any leftovers, they make for a real treat in the lunchbox the next day.

I've spoiled my kids when it comes to food and flavours, so they love chicken wings on this oriental risotto, but you could also serve them with fluffy rice or a green salad ... the possibilities are endless.

STICKY CHICKEN WINGS
115 g (4 oz/⅓ cup) honey
80 ml (2½ fl oz/⅓ cup) soy sauce
2 heaped tablespoons roughly chopped
    fresh ginger
2 tablespoons roughly chopped garlic
80 ml (2½ fl oz/⅓ cup) dry sherry or
    Chinese rice wine
drizzle of peanut or sesame oil
pinch of Chinese five spice
12 meaty chicken wings (free-range
    or organic, if you can)

RISOTTO
20 g (¾ oz) dried, sliced shiitake mushrooms
375 ml (13 fl oz/1½ cups) boiling water
60 ml (2 fl oz/¼ cup) peanut oil
1 tablespoon finely chopped garlic
1 tablespoon finely chopped fresh
    ginger
1 lemongrass stem, pale part only,
    finely chopped
100 g (3½ oz) red Asian shallots
    (about 4), finely chopped
330 g (11½ oz/1½ cups) arborio rice
2 tablespoons dry sherry or Chinese
    rice wine
1 litre (35 fl oz/4 cups) hot, good-quality
    chicken stock
sea salt and freshly ground black pepper
drizzle of soy sauce
50 g (1¾ oz) enoki mushrooms
2 spring onions (scallions), finely chopped
1 cup coriander (cilantro) leaves and
    stems, sliced

TO COOK THE CHICKEN WINGS

Blitz all of the ingredients (except the chicken) together in a food processor until smooth.

Pour the marinade over the chicken in a shallow dish, cover and refrigerate for at least 3 hours, or overnight, turning occasionally.

Preheat the oven to 190°C (375°F/Gas 5).

Tip the chicken and marinade into a non-stick roasting tray (or use a roasting tray lined with baking paper) and roast, turning halfway through, for 45 minutes to 1 hour, or until the wings are golden, sticky and a bit crispy.

Serve the chicken wings with the risotto and some steamed bok choy (pak choy).

TO COOK THE RISOTTO

Soak the shiitake mushrooms in the boiling water until softened.

Heat the peanut oil in a large heavy-based saucepan over low heat. Add the garlic, ginger, lemongrass and shallots and cook for 3–4 minutes, or until the shallots are translucent.

Add the rice and stir continuously until it is well coated and begins to stick.

Increase the heat to medium, then add the sherry, soaked shiitake mushrooms (including the water) and three-quarters of the hot stock (see Note). Stir occasionally.

Once the rice has absorbed most of the liquid, add the remaining stock, a ladle at a time, until the rice is just cooked through but still *al dente*. Taste for seasoning and add a drizzle of soy. The cooking time should be 15–20 minutes in total.

Just before serving, stir through the enoki mushrooms, spring onion and coriander.

NOTE Risotto purists won't be happy to hear this, but I simply stick most of my stock in at the beginning then walk away and do other things. If I walk by the pan, I might give it a stir, but I'm not into standing over it the whole time. The end result is still oozy, delicious risotto that goes beautifully with all sorts of things like steamed bok choy, tofu, shredded Chinese duck or even a seared piece of salmon.

cauliflower & squash cheese

Serves 6 as a side dish

I grew up on cauliflower cheese and sausages for dinner at least once a week so this recipe is an oldie but a goodie. Adding juicy yellow squash gives the dish a clean sweet burst of flavour to counter the rich creamy sauce.

TO MAKE THE BASIC CHEESE SAUCE

Preheat the oven to 180°C (350°F/Gas 4).

Heat the milk gently in a small saucepan with the nutmeg, salt and pepper.

Melt the butter in a heavy-based saucepan over low heat, then add the flour and stir continuously with a wooden spoon for about 2 minutes, or until it starts to bubble and turn a pale straw colour.

Whisk in the warm milk, then increase the heat to medium and bring slowly to the boil, stirring continuously until it thickens to a smooth sauce consistency.

Stir in the mustard, cheese and parsley. Once the cheese has melted, remove from the heat.

TO MAKE THE CAULIFLOWER CHEESE

Steam or boil the cauliflower for 10 minutes, or until cooked but still firm.

Add the squash halfway through the cooking time. Drain well.

Put the veggies into a shallow 30 x 25 cm (12 x 10 inch), 3.5 litre (122 fl oz/14 cup) capacity baking dish, pour the cheese sauce all over to cover the veggies completely then scatter the grated cheddar over the top.

Bake for 35 minutes, or until the cheese is golden and bubbling. Serve with your favourite cooked sausages (mine are German veal and chive sausages).

NOTE You can change up the cheese sauce by adding different flavours such as a little smoked paprika or horseradish cream.

INGREDIENTS

1 cauliflower, cut into florets

500 g (1 lb 2 oz) yellow baby squash (pattypan), halved

150 g (5½ oz/1¼ cups) grated cheddar cheese

BASIC CHEESE SAUCE

1 litre (35 fl oz/4 cups) milk

5 gratings of nutmeg

sea salt and freshly ground black pepper

125 g (4½ oz) butter

50 g (1¾ oz/⅓ cup) plain (all-purpose) flour

2 teaspoons dijon mustard

125 g (4½ oz/1¼ cups) grated cheddar cheese

½ cup flat-leaf (Italian) parsley leaves, chopped

hazelnut-crumbed pork chops

Serves 4

If I crumb it and fry it, my kids always love it! This is a gorgeous crumbing mixture; the addition of hazelnuts gives the chops extra flavour and texture. I usually serve it with cauliflower and squash cheese or simple steamed veg.

INGREDIENTS

115 g (4 oz/¾ cup) hazelnuts, roasted and peeled

30 g (1 oz/½ cup) breadcrumbs (I like to use panko/ Japanese breadcrumbs)

1 heaped teaspoon dijon mustard

4 pork chops, excess fat trimmed

1 egg

2 tablespoons milk

sea salt and freshly ground black pepper

2 tablespoons olive oil

20 g (¾ oz) unsalted butter

METHOD

Preheat the oven to 200°C (400°F/Gas 6).

Blitz the hazelnuts in a food processor until you have a fine crumble consistency, then mix with the breadcrumbs.

Rub the mustard all over the pork chops.

Whisk the egg and milk together in a bowl and season with salt and pepper. Dip the pork chops in the egg mixture, allowing the excess to drain off, then coat generously with the crumb mixture.

Heat the olive oil and butter in a large frying pan over medium–high heat. Add the pork chops and cook for a few minutes on each side, or until lightly golden.

Transfer the pork to a roasting tray and roast in the oven for 20 minutes, or until cooked through.

Serve the pork chops with the classic family favourite, cauliflower and squash cheese (see page 153).

creamy pesto & pea pasta with crispy pancetta

Serves 6

If you have pesto handy, this is a quick and simple pasta. Make sure you hide the crispy pancetta once it's cooked, as small children and lurking partners will devour it before you can get it into the finished dish!

FOR THE PASTA

Preheat the oven to 160°C (315°F/Gas 2–3).

Arrange the pancetta slices on a baking tray lined with baking paper. Cover with another sheet of baking paper and press together. This will keep the pancetta flat.

Bake for about 10 minutes, or until crisp, then put aside. In the meantime, make your pesto (see below).

Cook the pasta in a large saucepan of salted boiling water until *al dente*, then drain and return to the pan.

Meanwhile, gently heat the cream in a medium saucepan over low heat for about 5 minutes, or until it thickens a little and reduces by about one-third.

Add the frozen peas and cook for 1 minute, or until the cream comes back to the simmering point.

Stir in a ½ cup of the pesto.

Add the sauce to the pasta, season with salt and pepper and toss to combine well.

Serve the pasta with the crispy pancetta on top and sprinkle over lots of parmesan.

FOR THE PESTO

Blitz all of the ingredients in a food processor until smooth.

Store in a clean jar in the fridge covered with extra oil to stop discolouration. The pesto will make enough for 250 g (9 oz/1 cup), and it will keep for one week, but it always tastes best when it's fresh.

PASTA

200 g (7 oz) thinly sliced flat pancetta

650 g (1 lb 7 oz) spaghetti

300 ml (10½ fl oz) thin (pouring) cream

140 g (5 oz/1 cup) frozen peas

125 g (4½ oz/½ cup) pesto (see recipe below)

sea salt and freshly ground black pepper

coarsely grated parmesan cheese, to serve

PESTO

2 cups (firmly packed) basil leaves

¼ cup (firmly packed) flat-leaf (Italian) parsley leaves

80 g (2¾ oz/½ cup) pine nuts, lightly toasted

4 garlic cloves

30 g (1 oz/¼ cup) coarsely grated parmesan cheese

2 tablespoons lemon juice

80 ml (2½ fl oz/⅓ cup) olive oil, plus extra to cover

½ teaspoon sea salt

freshly ground black pepper

sweet things

I started cooking when I was little. I grew up in a healthy, hippie household full of lentils and silverbeet, but I had a sweet tooth. Once I learned I could conjure beautiful treats from the sugary odds and ends in the pantry, get to lick the bowl *and* be a hero to my brothers and sister at the same time, I was hooked. I've never stopped enjoying the wow factor of serving people sweet things. Everybody loves a treat: kids can't help themselves, grown-ups know better and just serve themselves half a piece (three times) and Granny and Pop are shameless.

Dessert is simple and honest. It makes no pretence of being healthy and offers no apology to the waistline. It has a direct, unwavering purpose: to make us feel good. The desserts in this chapter are a combination of old family favourites and the current manifestations of my sweet obsessions.

chocolate, fig & hazelnut torte

Serves 10–12

Even those who don't generally like to indulge in desserts seem to find this one irresistibly enticing. Sometimes I like to serve it warm while the chocolate is still deliciously gooey.

INGREDIENTS

butter, for greasing

250 g (9 oz) soft dried figs, stems removed, cut into 1 cm (½ inch) pieces

pinch of ground cinnamon

125 ml (4 fl oz/½ cup) Frangelico, or other hazelnut-flavoured liqueur

300 g (10½ oz) good-quality dark chocolate (70% cocoa solids)

250 g (9 oz) hazelnuts, roasted and peeled

6 egg whites

100 g (3½ oz) caster (superfine) sugar

icing (confectioners') sugar, for dusting

unsweetened cocoa powder, for dusting

double (thick) cream, to serve

METHOD

Preheat the oven to 160°C (315°F/Gas 2–3) and arrange an oven rack on the middle shelf.

Grease and line the base of a 26 cm (10½ inch) spring-form cake tin with baking paper.

Soak the figs with the cinnamon in the Frangelico while you prepare the remaining ingredients.

Roughly chop the chocolate and hazelnuts (by hand or in a food processor), then add to the soaking figs.

Whisk the egg whites using an electric mixer fitted with a whisk attachment until stiff peaks form.

Leave the mixer running and gradually add the caster sugar, whisking until thick and glossy.

Fold the egg white mixture into the fig mixture until combined. Spoon into the prepared tin and bake for 45 minutes, or until just firm. Cool slightly before removing from the tin.

Serve the torte warm or cold, dusted with icing sugar and cocoa powder, with some cream on the side.

pear & rhubarb crumble

Serves 6

My friend Tansy inspired this recipe. She is an excellent home cook and the only dessert she ever makes is rhubarb crumble. There's something homely and humble about a sweet and tart crumble.

METHOD
Preheat the oven to 180°C (350°F/Gas 4).

TO MAKE THE CRUMBLE FILLING
Heat the butter and sugar in a wide heavy-based saucepan over medium heat until melted and the mixture just starts to bubble together and caramelise.
Add the fruit, cinnamon and vanilla bean and seeds to the saucepan, stir to combine and cook over low heat for a few minutes.
Add the wine and cook for 5 minutes, or until the fruit is half cooked. Pour into a 30 x 20 cm (12 x 8 inch), 2.5 litre (87 fl oz/10 cup) capacity baking dish.

TO MAKE THE CRUMBLE TOPPING
Rub the butter, sugar and flour together in a bowl with your fingertips until the mixture resembles a crumble consistency.
Stir in the almond meal and flaked almonds until combined.

TO ASSEMBLE AND COOK THE CRUMBLE
Sprinkle the crumble over the fruit mixture.
Bake for 30 minutes, or until the crumble is golden on top.
Serve hot with a scoop of good-quality vanilla-bean ice cream.

NOTE You can use whatever fruit is in season for this. Softer fruit needs less pre-cooking time and requires less wine as it will not reduce as much.

CRUMBLE FILLING
50 g (1¾ oz) unsalted butter
165 g (5¾ oz/¾ cup) caster (superfine) sugar
600 g (1 lb 5 oz) trimmed rhubarb (about 2 bunches), washed and cut into 3 cm (1¼ inch) pieces (see Note)
6 pears, peeled, cored and cut into 6 wedges each (see Note)
pinch of ground cinnamon
½ a vanilla bean, halved lengthways, seeds scraped
185 ml (6 fl oz/¾ cup) white wine (or verjuice for a non-alcoholic version)
vanilla-bean ice cream, to serve

CRUMBLE TOPPING
150 g (5½ oz) cold unsalted butter, finely diced
110 g (3¾ oz/½ cup) caster (superfine) sugar
150 g (5½ oz/1 cup) plain (all-purpose) flour
100 g (3½ oz/1 cup) almond meal (ground almonds)
30 g (1 oz) flaked almonds

baci cake

Serves 12

This cake is deceivingly light, but loaded with lots of naughty stuff. It is inspired by a lovely friend of mine Debbie Gyde who makes wicked cakes. This only makes an appearance on special occasions in our house, and my son's birthday parties are well attended because of it.

MERINGUE
unsalted butter, for greasing
210 g (7½ oz/1½ cups) hazelnuts, roasted
    and peeled
30 g (1 oz/¼ cup) cornflour (cornstarch)
275 g (9¾ oz/1¼ cups) caster (superfine) sugar
10 egg whites

CHOCOLATE CREAM
500 g (1 lb 2 oz/3⅓ cups) dark chocolate
    melts (buttons), roughly chopped
250 ml (9 fl oz/1 cup) thin (pouring) cream
180 g (6¼ oz) unsalted butter, diced, at room
    temperature

TO SERVE
270 g (9½ oz/2 cups) hazelnuts, roasted
    and peeled, for decorating

TO MAKE THE MERINGUE

Preheat the oven to 140°C (275°F/Gas 1).

Grease and line three baking trays or 25 cm (10 inch) pizza trays with baking paper. Using a 20 cm (8 inch) round plate or bowl as a guide, trace three circles onto each piece of baking paper.

Put the hazelnuts in a food processor and pulse until coarsely ground.

Add the cornflour and 55 g (2 oz/¼ cup) of the sugar and pulse until well combined.

Whisk the egg whites in an electric mixer fitted with a whisk attachment until stiff peaks form, then gradually add the remaining sugar and whisk until stiff and glossy.

Fold in the hazelnut mixture with a large metal spoon until combined.

Divide the meringue mixture equally between the three prepared trays. Use a palette knife to make three smooth 20 cm (8 inch) diameter circles, about 2.5 cm (1 inch) high.

Bake for 1 hour, rotating the trays after 30 minutes so the meringues cook evenly.

Turn off the oven and allow the meringues to cool in the oven for 30 minutes, then remove from the oven and allow to cool completely.

TO MAKE THE CHOCOLATE CREAM

Melt the chocolate and cream together over a double boiler, or on a gentle heat in the microwave until well combined and smooth. Remove from the heat and allow to cool.

Whisk the cooled chocolate mixture on a high speed using an electric mixer while slowly adding the butter. The mixture should be thick, smooth and creamy. If it's a little runny, put it in the fridge for 30 minutes, then whisk again until thick and smooth.

TO ASSEMBLE

Carefully peel the baking paper off the bases of the meringues.

Place a meringue on a big round serving platter and spread 2 generous spoonfuls of the chocolate cream evenly over the top.

Place a second meringue on top and repeat with the chocolate cream.

Put the last meringue on top and cover the entire cake with the remaining chocolate cream.

Pulse the remaining hazelnuts in a food processor four times until roughly chopped, but still chunky.

Gently press the chopped hazelnuts all around the side and top of the cake so it's completely coated. It's easiest to do this with your hands.

Chill for 30 minutes before serving. The cake will keep for up to three days in the fridge.

apple & strawberry pie

Serves 8

Short and buttery, floral and sweet, this apple and strawberry pie is always a hit. Never underestimate the importance of a good short pastry.

SHORTCRUST PASTRY
300 g (10½ oz/2 cups) plain (all-purpose) flour
150 g (5½ oz/1 cup) self-raising flour
250 g (9 oz) cold unsalted butter,
    finely diced
150 g (5½ oz/⅔ cup) caster (superfine) sugar
½ teaspoon vanilla bean paste
4 egg yolks
2 tablespoons cold water

PIE FILLING
7 granny smith (green) apples
    (about 850 g/1 lb 14 oz), peeled
2 tablespoons caster (superfine) sugar
2 tablespoons water
500 g (1 lb 2 oz/3½ cups) strawberries,
    washed, hulled and halved

TO SERVE
icing (confectioners') sugar, for dusting
vanilla-bean ice cream

METHOD
Preheat the oven to 180°C (350°F/Gas 4).

TO MAKE THE SHORTCRUST PASTRY
Pulse the flours, butter and sugar five or six times in a food processor until the mixture resembles breadcrumbs.
Whisk the vanilla bean paste, egg yolks and cold water together with a fork. Add to the flour mixture and pulse three or four times, or until the pastry just starts to come together.
Tip the pastry into a bowl and bring it together with your hands to make a smooth ball. The trick here is to gather it all up and bind it without overworking it.
Divide the pastry in half, wrap each piece in plastic wrap and refrigerate for 30 minutes.

TO MAKE THE PIE FILLING
Quarter the apples, then core and cut into rough pieces. Put in a large saucepan over medium heat, sprinkle with the caster sugar and water, then cover with a lid and cook for about 5 minutes.
Remove the lid, increase the heat to high and continue cooking for a few more minutes, or until the apple has absorbed all of the juices in the pan. The fruit should only be half cooked. Remove the pan from the heat, add the strawberries and set aside to cool.

TO ASSEMBLE AND COOK THE PIE
Roll each piece of pastry between two sheets of baking paper into a 30–32 cm (12–12¾ inch) round.
Peel the top sheet of baking paper from one pastry round and put the pastry onto a large baking tray. Spoon the cooled fruit over the pastry base, leaving a 3 cm (1¼ inch) border.
Peel the top sheet of baking paper from the other pastry round and carefully place the pastry lid over the pie. Remove the baking paper then fold over the edge of the pastry to enclose the pie and seal the edges together using your fingers or a fork. Prick the top of the pie to allow the steam to escape.
Bake for 35–40 minutes, or until the pastry is light golden.
Dust with icing sugar while still warm and serve with ice cream. It's also delicious cold the next day.

pistachio & apricot bread

Makes about 40 slices

The first time I made this bread I couldn't believe how easy and rewarding it was. Gourmet wafer crispbreads are so expensive to buy and this loaf makes enough for a party!

INGREDIENTS

butter, for greasing

3 egg whites

110 g (3¾ oz/½ cup) caster (superfine) sugar

150 g (5½ oz/1 cup) plain (all-purpose) flour, sifted

210 g (7½ oz/1½ cups) pistachio nuts

75 g (2½ oz/½ cup) finely chopped dried apricots

METHOD

Preheat the oven to 170°C (325°F/Gas 3).

Grease a 1.25 litre (44 fl oz/5 cup) capacity loaf (bar) tin and line the base and two long sides with baking paper.

Whisk the egg whites using an electric mixer fitted with a whisk attachment until soft peaks form.

Leave the mixer running and gradually add the sugar. Whisk until the mixture is glossy and the sugar has dissolved.

Fold in the flour, pistachios and apricots then pour into the prepared tin.

Bake for 40 minutes, then test with a cake skewer. If it comes out clean, it's ready. Allow to cool completely in the tin. (I usually allow my loaf to sit overnight as it dries out a little and is easier to slice thinly.)

Preheat the oven to 120°C (235°F/Gas ½).

Remove the bread from the tin and thinly slice using a serrated knife.

Arrange the slices flat on baking trays lined with baking paper and bake for 15 minutes, or until completely dried out and just golden.

Remove from the oven and allow to cool completely on the trays. Store in an airtight container for up to three weeks.

rosy raspberry peaches

Serves 15

When freestone peaches are in season, this is a quick and cheeky last-minute dessert for a crowd. It also looks spectacular served in a beautiful punchbowl.

METHOD

Put the sugar, wine and cinnamon (if using) in a large saucepan over medium heat with the water and simmer for about 10 minutes, or until the sugar has dissolved.

Add the raspberries, reduce the heat to low and simmer for 10 minutes, or until the raspberries start to break down and the mixture turns a lovely blushing red.

Remove from the heat and add the rose syrup.

Add the peaches and leave them in the syrup as it cools (see Notes).

Serve the poached peach halves with a little of their syrup and a spoonful of ice cream or cream.

NOTES Rose syrup is available from continental delicatessens.

Store the peaches in a glass bowl in the fridge covered with a cartouche (or plastic wrap pressed directly onto the surface) to stop them from discolouring. If there are any leftovers, they're great the next day for breakfast with yoghurt.

INGREDIENTS

220 g (7¾ oz/1 cup) caster (superfine) sugar

250 ml (9 fl oz/1 cup) white wine

1 cinnamon stick (optional)

700 ml (24 fl oz) water

360 g (12¾ oz) frozen raspberries

2 tablespoons rose syrup (see Notes)

15 freestone (slipstone) white peaches, halved and stones removed

ice cream or thickened (whipping) cream, to serve

three fruit flans

Each flan serves 6–8

Why make one flan when you can make three in one go? These flans can be made with any fruit in season. They're great for picnics or large gatherings, and they look fabulous served side-by-side on a big chopping board.

INGREDIENTS

60 g (2¼ oz) unsalted butter,
    softened, for greasing
3 heaped tablespoons caster
    (superfine) sugar, for dusting
icing (confectioners') sugar,
    for dusting

BATTER

450 g (1 lb) unsalted butter,
    diced and softened
450 g (1 lb) caster
    (superfine) sugar
1 teaspoon vanilla bean paste
4 large eggs
450 g (1 lb/4½ cups) almond meal
    (ground almonds)
4½ heaped tablespoons
    self-raising flour

FRUIT

4 plump red tamarillos, peeled
    and cut into thick slices
6 apricots, halved and stones
    removed
300 g (10½ oz/1½ cups) morello
    cherries, well-drained and
    stones removed

METHOD

Preheat the oven to 180°C (350°F/Gas 4) and arrange an oven rack on the middle shelf.

Grease three 35 x 12 cm (14 x 4½ inch) loose-based tart (flan) tins. Line the base and sides of each tin with foil or baking paper, being careful not to pierce the lining.

Rub each lined tin with one-third of the butter and sprinkle 1 heaped tablespoon of caster sugar evenly over each tray.

TO MAKE THE BATTER

Beat the butter, sugar and vanilla bean paste using an electric mixer until light and creamy.

Leave the mixer running and beat in the eggs one at a time.

Use a spoon to fold in the almond meal and flour until well combined.

TO MAKE AND SERVE THE FLANS

Arrange the fruit in the prepared trays, spreading the tamarillo slices evenly around one, the apricot halves (cut side down) around another, and the cherries all over the base of the third.

Divide the batter evenly between the three flans, spreading it evenly over the fruit.

Bake on the middle shelf of the oven for 45 minutes, or until the flans are firm and golden on top.

Remove from the oven and allow to cool slightly.

Place a flat platter or board over each flan and turn upside down, and then remove the tins.

Dust with icing sugar then serve.

butterfly cupcakes

Makes 18

When I make these pretty little cakes I think of granny gatherings, crocheted tea cosies and endless cups of tea. My grandmother used to fill these with lemon curd and cream, but a homemade jam is equally delicious, and often handy in the pantry.

METHOD

Preheat the oven to 180°C (350°F/Gas 4). Line two 12-hole (80 ml/2½ fl oz/⅓ cup capacity) muffin tins with paper cases (you'll only need to prepare 18 of the muffin holes).

Sift the flour into a bowl.

Beat the butter, caster sugar and vanilla bean paste together until light and creamy.

Beat in the eggs, one at a time, adding a spoonful of the flour to stop the mixture from separating.

Fold in the remaining flour and milk until well combined.

Spoon the mixture into the paper cases, filling each one about three-quarters full.

Bake for 15–20 minutes, or until just golden and cooked through.

Remove from the oven and transfer to a wire rack to cool completely.

Use a small sharp knife to carefully cut out 3 cm (1¼ inch) diameter circles, about 2 cm (¾ inch) deep from the centre of each cake. When doing this, point the tip of the knife towards the centre of the cake so it follows the narrowing line of the cupcake. Reserve the cupcake tops.

Spoon 1 teaspoon of jam into each lined hole, then top with a generous dollop of cream.

Cut the reserved tops in half and arrange over the cream to form wings.

Serve dusted with icing sugar.

INGREDIENTS

280 g (10 oz) self-raising flour

170 g (5¾ oz) unsalted butter, softened

170 g (5¾ oz) caster (superfine) sugar

½ teaspoon vanilla bean paste

4 eggs

125 ml (4 fl oz/½ cup) milk

85 g (3 oz/¼ cup) raspberry jam

150 ml (5 fl oz) thickened (whipping) cream, whipped

icing (confectioners') sugar, for dusting

icky sticky figgy puddings

Makes 8

Wintertime is pudding time. These figgy delights are delicious straight out of the oven with a spoonful of naughty butterscotch sauce and a generous dollop of cream. They'll keep for up to five days in the fridge and they freeze well, too. To reheat, you can microwave the puddings on a medium heat with the sauce over the top. This makes them extra moist.

FIGGY PUDDINGS

100 g (3½ oz) unsalted butter, diced and
    softened, plus extra for greasing
250 g (9 oz) soft dried figs, stems removed
300 ml (10½ fl oz) water
1 teaspoon bicarbonate of soda (baking soda)
250 g (9 oz) soft brown sugar
3 eggs
250 g (9 oz/1⅔ cups) self-raising flour
pinch of ground cinnamon
ice cream or thin (pouring) cream, to serve

NAUGHTY BUTTERSCOTCH SAUCE

100 g (3½ oz) unsalted butter
300 g (10½ oz) soft brown sugar
60 ml (2 fl oz/¼ cup) brandy (optional)
250 ml (9 fl oz/1 cup) thin (pouring)
    cream or water

TO MAKE THE PUDDINGS

Preheat the oven to 200°C (400°F/Gas 6).

Grease eight 250 ml (9 fl oz/1 cup) capacity coffee cups or moulds.

Roughly chop the figs and put them into a large heavy-based saucepan with the water and bicarbonate of soda. Bring to the boil, then simmer over low heat for 5 minutes, or until the figs have softened.

Remove from the heat, then stir in the butter until melted.

Add the sugar and stir until dissolved.

Lightly beat the eggs, then add them to the mixture with the flour and cinnamon, and stir to combine (see Note).

Pour into the prepared cups. Put the cups into a large roasting tray and pour in enough water to come halfway up the sides of the cups. Cover the tray with foil, sealing the edges well so the steam can't escape.

Bake for 45 minutes.

TO MAKE THE BUTTERSCOTCH SAUCE

Melt the butter and sugar in a saucepan over low–medium heat, stirring until the sugar dissolves and the mixture bubbles.

Remove from the heat and carefully stir in the brandy (if using).

Return to the heat and stir in the cream until the sauce is a smooth consistency then keep warm until ready to serve.

TO SERVE THE PUDDINGS

Turn the puddings out of their cups, pour over the sauce and serve with ice cream or a drizzle of cream.

NOTE If you're a nut freak like me, try adding some chopped pecans to the pudding batter.

tealight chocolate mousse with pistachio praline

Makes 8

This will take 20 minutes to whip up, two minutes to eat, half an hour to jog off and by that time you will be ready for another one! These are great little sweet treats to serve at a party and they look really pretty served in small glass tealight holders or shot glasses.

CHOCOLATE MOUSSE

300 g (10½ oz) good-quality dark chocolate
   (70% cocoa solids), roughly chopped
4 eggs, separated
40 g (1½ oz) caster (superfine) sugar
2 teaspoons Cointreau or other
   orange-flavoured liqueur (optional)
pinch of ground cinnamon
1 teaspoon finely grated orange zest
200 ml (7 fl oz) thin (pouring) cream
thickened (whipping) cream, whipped,
   to serve

PISTACHIO PRALINE

150 g (5½ oz/⅔ cup) caster (superfine) sugar
80 ml (2½ fl oz/⅓ cup) water
1 teaspoon lemon juice
35 g (1¼ oz/¼ cup) pistachio nut kernels

TO MAKE THE CHOCOLATE MOUSSE

Melt the chocolate over a double boiler (or on a gentle heat in the microwave) until smooth. Stir at 30-second intervals to avoid overcooking. Allow to cool.

Combine the egg yolks, sugar, Cointreau (if using), cinnamon and orange zest in a large stainless-steel bowl until smooth.

Add the cooled melted chocolate to the mixture and stir until well combined.

Whip the thin cream until soft peaks form.

Beat the egg whites until soft peaks form.

Gently fold the whisked egg white and whipped cream together. Fold one-third into the chocolate mixture until well combined.

Gently fold in the remaining egg white mixture until there are no streaks.

Divide between the tealight holders and refrigerate for 2 hours, or until set.

TO MAKE THE PISTACHIO PRALINE

Put the sugar, water and lemon juice in a small heavy-based saucepan and bring to the boil over low heat, stirring a few times until the sugar has dissolved.

Increase the heat to high and bring to the boil, then continue to cook for about 5 minutes without stirring. Brush down the side of the pan with a pastry brush dipped in water to dissolve any sugar crystals. When it turns a golden toffee colour, it is ready. Do not be tempted to taste or touch the caramel at any point — it is very hot and can burn.

Remove from the heat immediately, allow the bubbles to settle, then add the pistachios and pour onto a tray lined with baking paper to cool and harden.

Chop the cooled praline to a fine consistency by hand or in a food processor. Store in an airtight container until ready to serve.

TO SERVE

Spoon a dollop of whipped cream on top of each mousse and finish with a sprinkle of pistachio praline.

lemon lime puddings

Makes 6

Some of the best recipes are handed down from generation to generation. This one has been in our family since before anyone can remember.

METHOD

Preheat the oven to 180°C (350°F/Gas 4).

Grease six 300 ml (10½ fl oz) capacity ramekins (or one 1.5 litre/52 fl oz/6 cup capacity ceramic baking dish).

Use an electric mixer to beat the butter, sugar and citrus zest until light and creamy.

Add the egg yolks and combine well, then add the flour and milk alternately and mix until a smooth batter forms.

Add the citrus juices to the batter and mix to lightly combine.

Whisk the egg whites with hand-held electric beaters or use a clean electric mixer fitted with a whisk attachment until stiff peaks form.

Fold the whisked egg white into the pudding batter. Divide between the prepared ramekins (or dish), put into a deep roasting tray, then pour in enough hot water to come halfway up the sides of the ramekins.

Bake for 20 minutes (or 30–40 minutes for one large pudding), or until the puddings are golden on top and still slightly springy.

Serve immediately with a little drizzle of cream, if you like.

INGREDIENTS

130 g (4½ oz) unsalted butter, plus extra for greasing

220 g (7¾ oz/1 cup) caster (superfine) sugar

finely grated zest and juice of 2 limes

finely grated zest and juice of 1 large lemon

4 large eggs, separated

75 g (2½ oz/⅓ cup) self-raising flour, sifted

500 ml (17 fl oz/2 cups) milk

thin (pouring) cream, to serve (optional)

almond & clove shortbreads

Makes 25

My fairy food godmother, Pauline, insisted I put cloves in my shortbread. As always, it was a genius suggestion and it has given them new life.

INGREDIENTS

200 g (7 oz) unsalted butter, softened

75 g (2½ oz/⅓ cup) caster (superfine) sugar

1 egg yolk

1 teaspoon rosewater or natural vanilla extract

300 g (10½ oz/2 cups) plain (all-purpose) flour

½ teaspoon baking powder

160 g (5¾ oz/1 cup) blanched almonds, toasted and blitzed to a crumbly consistency

25 whole cloves

125 g (4½ oz/1 cup) icing (confectioners') sugar, for dusting

METHOD

Preheat the oven to 170°C (325°F/Gas 3) and line a large baking tray with baking paper.

Beat the butter and caster sugar together until light and creamy.

Add the egg yolk and rosewater (or vanilla extract) and beat in well.

Sift in the flour and baking powder.

Fold in the almonds and mix until well combined.

Roll the mixture into small walnut-sized balls.

Arrange on the prepared tray and gently flatten each shortbread with two fingers.

Poke a clove into the centre of each shortbread.

Bake for 15–20 minutes, or until light golden.

Move the shortbreads to a wire rack to cool slightly, and dust with icing sugar to coat while still warm.

banana toffee tart

Serves 8

This gorgeous dessert is the lovechild of banoffee pie and cheesecake. I like to think it's inherited the best features from both sides of the family.

BASE
125 g (4½ oz) unsalted butter, melted,
    plus extra for greasing
300 g (10½ oz) spiced speculaas biscuits
    (cookies) (see Note)
180 g (6¼ oz) good-quality dark chocolate
    (70% cocoa solids), chopped and melted

FILLING
250 ml (9 fl oz/1 cup) thin (pouring) cream
250 g (9 oz) mascarpone cheese,
    at room temperature
1 tablespoon honey
1 teaspoon natural vanilla extract
5 large firm, ripe bananas

CHOCOLATE GANACHE TOPPING
50 g (1¾ oz) good-quality dark chocolate
    (70% cocoa solids), chopped
2 tablespoons thin (pouring) cream

TOFFEE PECAN TOPPING
165 g (5¾ oz/¾ cup) caster (superfine) sugar
125 ml (4 fl oz/½ cup) water
50 g (1¾ oz/½ cup) pecans

METHOD
Preheat the oven to 180°C (350°F/Gas 4).
Grease a 25 cm (10 inch) loose-based round fluted tart (flan) tin and line the base with baking paper.

TO MAKE THE BASE
Blitz the biscuits in a food processor until you have fine crumbs. Add the melted butter and mix together until combined.
Press the biscuit mixture evenly over the base and up the side of the tin, pressing it firmly with your hands to ensure it is solid.
Bake for 10 minutes. Remove from the oven and cool completely in the tin to set.
Spread the melted chocolate over the base and side of the cooled tart case (still in the tin).
Refrigerate the tart case until the chocolate has completely chilled.
When ready to fill, carefully remove the case from the tart tin, peel off the baking paper and put the tart case on a serving plate.

TO MAKE THE FILLING

Beat the cream, mascarpone, honey and vanilla extract together using an electric mixer until lightly combined and the consistency of whipped cream. Do not overmix.
Spread the filling over the chocolate biscuit base.
Cut the bananas into 1.5 cm ($\frac{5}{8}$ inch) thick rounds and push them into the cream mixture to completely cover. Pop in the fridge until ready to top.

TO MAKE THE CHOCOLATE GANACHE TOPPING

Melt the chocolate and cream together over a double boiler (or on a gentle heat in the microwave) until well combined and smooth, then remove from the heat and allow to cool slightly.

TO MAKE THE TOFFEE PECAN TOPPING

Put the sugar and water in a small heavy-based saucepan and bring to the boil over low heat. Gently stir a few times until the sugar has dissolved.
Increase the heat to high and, once boiling, continue to cook, without stirring, for 4–5 minutes. Brush down the side of the pan with a pastry brush dipped in water to dissolve any sugar crystals. When it turns a golden toffee colour, it is ready. Do not be tempted to taste or touch the caramel at any point — it is very hot and can burn.
Remove from the heat immediately, allow the bubbles to settle, then add the pecans and pour the mixture onto a tray lined with baking paper to cool and harden.
Chop the hardened praline to a chunky consistency.

TO TOP THE TART

Drizzle two-thirds of the ganache topping over the banana cream filling, top with the toffee pecans, then drizzle the remaining ganache over the top.
Refrigerate for at least 30 minutes before serving.

NOTE You can also use any plain sweet biscuits for this base, just as you would for a cheesecake. Just add a pinch of cinnamon to spice things up!

fruit salad with spiced syrup

Serves 4–6

The best thing about fruit salad is that it's so easy to whip up, and you can make the most out of any slightly sad-looking fruit that you've neglected in the fridge or fruit bowl. I like to gloss mine up with a spiced sugar syrup. It can turn an underrated dessert into a stunning after-dinner delight! I'm crazy for orange blossom water at the moment, but it's an acquired taste so I've also included a luscious lemongrass syrup, which works really well with tropical fruit.

FRUIT SALAD

1 red apple, peeled and cut into rounds
1 kiwi fruit, peeled and cut into rounds
1 orange, peeled and thinly sliced
1 ruby red grapefruit, peeled
    and segmented
piece of watermelon, peeled and sliced
piece of pineapple, peeled and sliced
1 pear, cored, halved and sliced
250 g (9 oz/1⅔ cups) strawberries, washed,
    hulled and cut into 3 slices each
double (thick) cream, to serve

SPICED ORANGE BLOSSOM SYRUP

110 g (3¾ oz/½ cup) caster (superfine) sugar
½ a vanilla bean, halved lengthways,
    seeds scraped
2 cardamom pods, bruised
125 ml (4 fl oz/½ cup) water
125 ml (4 fl oz/½ cup) freshly squeezed
    orange juice
juice of 1 lemon
1 teaspoon orange blossom water

LEMONGRASS & PASSIONFRUIT SYRUP

70 g (2½ oz/⅓ cup) grated palm sugar (jaggery)
125 ml (4 fl oz/½ cup) water
1 lemongrass stem, halved lengthways
    and tied in a knot
3 thin slices fresh peeled ginger
juice of 1 lime, strained
pulp of 2 passionfruit

TO MAKE THE SPICED ORANGE BLOSSOM SYRUP

Put the sugar, vanilla bean and seeds, and cardamom in a small heavy-based saucepan with the water and cook over medium heat for 5–10 minutes, or until the mixture becomes clear and is a thick syrupy consistency.

Stir in the orange and lemon juice, and the orange blossom water.

Strain through a fine sieve and cool.

TO MAKE THE LEMONGRASS AND PASSIONFRUIT SYRUP

Put the palm sugar, water, lemongrass and ginger in a small heavy-based saucepan over medium heat and cook for 5–10 minutes, or until the mixture becomes clear and is a thick syrupy consistency.

Stir in the lime juice and passionfruit pulp.

Cool, then remove the lemongrass and ginger (see Note).

TO SERVE THE FRUIT SALAD

Prepare the fruits and arrange them beautifully on a large platter with a lip.

Drizzle your choice of syrup all over the fruit, then cover and refrigerate until needed.

Serve with a bowl of cream on the side.

NOTE Instead of discarding the ginger slices from the lemongrass syrup, you can try slicing them very thinly into matchsticks and stirring those through the double cream before serving.

raspberry & rose meringues

Makes 8

Kids and adults love making, cooking and eating these. They're great for a lovely lunch day!

INGREDIENTS

4 egg whites

220 g (7¾ oz/1 cup) caster
(superfine) sugar

1 teaspoon white vinegar

1 teaspoon cornflour (cornstarch)

2 teaspoons rose syrup (see Note)

1 tablespoon hot water

¼ teaspoon natural vanilla extract

200 ml (7 fl oz) thickened
(whipping) cream, whipped,
to serve

fresh raspberries, to serve

icing (confectioners') sugar
(optional), to serve

METHOD

Preheat the oven to 120°C (235°F/Gas ½) and arrange an oven rack on the middle shelf. Line a large baking tray with baking paper.

Whisk the egg whites, sugar, vinegar, cornflour, rose syrup, hot water and vanilla extract together using an electric mixer on high speed for 10 minutes, or until the mixture is stiff and glossy.

Spoon onto the prepared tray to make eight meringue nests, about 6–8 cm (2½–3¼ inches) in diameter.

Bake for 40 minutes, then turn the oven off and allow the meringues to cool in the oven. They should be crunchy on the outside and like marshmallow on the inside.

To serve, top the meringues with the whipped cream and raspberries, and dust with a little icing sugar, if you like. You can always start the diet tomorrow!

NOTE Rose syrup is available from continental delicatessens.

chocolate & hazelnut cookies

Makes about 40

There's a reason most cookbooks have chocolate chip cookie recipes in them: they are such a beloved childhood classic, and there are as many different recipes for them as there are families in the world. Every kid must think their mum's recipe is the best — I know mine do!

While we were filming 'The Great Australian Bake Off', we gave twenty journos the same cookie recipe to bake and we got twenty different results! Once you start making your own cookies there's no turning back; the factory ones will taste like cardboard. Everyone should have a good cookie recipe up their sleeve.

METHOD

Preheat the oven to 180°C (350°F/Gas 4).

Line two large baking trays with baking paper.

Beat the butter, sugars and vanilla extract together in an electric mixer until light and really creamy.

Leave the mixer running, add the egg and beat in well.

Fold in the flours, nuts and chocolate until well combined.

Roll the mixture into a long sausage shape then wrap in plastic wrap and pop in the fridge for about 30 minutes to firm up.

Cut the cookie dough into 1 cm ($\frac{1}{2}$ inch) thick rounds and put on the prepared trays, allowing room for the cookies to spread a little.

Bake for 15–20 minutes, or until light golden. Allow to cool on the trays a little, then transfer to a wire rack to cool completely.

INGREDIENTS

200 g (7 oz) unsalted butter

100 g ($3\frac{1}{2}$ oz/$\frac{1}{2}$ cup, lightly packed) soft brown sugar

110 g ($3\frac{3}{4}$ oz/$\frac{1}{2}$ cup) caster (superfine) sugar

1 teaspoon natural vanilla extract

1 egg

225 g (8 oz/$1\frac{1}{2}$ cups) self-raising flour

75 g ($2\frac{1}{2}$ oz/$\frac{1}{2}$ cup) plain (all-purpose) flour

115 g (4 oz/$\frac{3}{4}$ cup) hazelnuts, roasted, peeled and coarsely chopped

150 g ($5\frac{1}{2}$ oz/1 cup) dark chocolate melts (buttons), roughly chopped

index

Page numbers in *italics* indicate photographs

conversion chart

oven temperature

°C	°F	gas
70	150	$\frac{1}{4}$
100	200	$\frac{1}{2}$
110	225	$\frac{1}{2}$
120	235	$\frac{1}{2}$
130	250	1
140	275	1
150	300	2
160	315	2–3
170	325	3
180	350	4
190	375	5
200	400	6
210	415	6–7
220	425	7
230	450	8
240	475	8
250	500	9

length

cm	inches
2 mm	$\frac{1}{16}$
3 mm	$\frac{1}{8}$
5 mm	$\frac{1}{4}$
8 mm	$\frac{3}{8}$
1	$\frac{1}{2}$
1.5	$\frac{5}{8}$
2	$\frac{3}{4}$
2.5	1
3	$1\frac{1}{4}$
4	$1\frac{1}{2}$
5	2
6	$2\frac{1}{2}$
7	$2\frac{3}{4}$
7.5	3
8	$3\frac{1}{4}$
9	$3\frac{1}{2}$
10	4
11	$4\frac{1}{4}$
12	$4\frac{1}{2}$
13	5
14	$5\frac{1}{2}$
15	6
16	$6\frac{1}{4}$
17	$6\frac{1}{2}$
18	7
19	$7\frac{1}{2}$
20	8
21	$8\frac{1}{4}$
22	$8\frac{1}{2}$
23	9
24	$9\frac{1}{2}$
25	10
30	12
35	14
40	16
45	$17\frac{3}{4}$
50	20

weight

g	oz
5	$\frac{1}{8}$
10	$\frac{1}{4}$
15	$\frac{1}{2}$
20	$\frac{3}{4}$
30	1
35	$1\frac{1}{4}$
40	$1\frac{1}{2}$
50	$1\frac{3}{4}$
55	2
60	$2\frac{1}{4}$
70	$2\frac{1}{2}$
80	$2\frac{3}{4}$
85	3
90	$3\frac{1}{4}$
100	$3\frac{1}{2}$
115	4
120	$4\frac{1}{4}$
125	$4\frac{1}{2}$
140	5
150	$5\frac{1}{2}$
175	6
200	7
225	8
250	9
280	10
300	$10\frac{1}{2}$
350	12
375	13
400	14
450	1 lb
500	1 lb 2 oz
550	1 lb 4 oz
600	1 lb 5 oz
700	1 lb 9 oz
800	1 lb 12 oz
900	2 lb
1 kg	2 lb 3 oz

liquid

ml	fl oz
30	1
60	2
80	$2\frac{1}{2}$
100	$3\frac{1}{2}$
125	4
160	$5\frac{1}{2}$
185	6
200	7
250	9
300	$10\frac{1}{2}$
350	12
375	13
400	14
500	17
600	21
650	$22\frac{1}{2}$
700	24
750	26
800	28
1 L	35
1.25 L	44
1.5 L	52

acknowledgements

Firstly, I would like to thank the people that have helped me make this book:

My husband, Luc Longley, for his overall contribution.

Ian Wallace and Louise Pickford for the beautiful photos.

Christine Osmond and Grace Campbell for proofing, testing and cooking all my recipes.

Katie Bosher for the final edit, and Hugh Ford for the fabulous book design.

Everyone at Murdoch Books and Allen & Unwin for helping me to produce another cookbook I am really proud of.

Thanks also to my very clever food friends Ursula Nairn and Suzy Foster for helping out with my recipe testing, and Tania King for the endless cups of tea — and for helping me to finally finish this book.

Now I'd like to thank the people who were my most willing accomplices — they consumed everything in this book. My darling hungry husband and our children: Jackson, Elsie, Lily and Clare.

Published in 2013 by Murdoch Books, an imprint of Allen & Unwin.

Murdoch Books Australia
83 Alexander Street
Crows Nest NSW 2065
Phone: +61 (0) 2 8425 0100
Fax: +61 (0) 2 9906 2218
www.murdochbooks.com.au
info@murdochbooks.com.au

Murdoch Books UK
Erico House, 6th Floor
93–99 Upper Richmond Road
Putney, London SW15 2TG
Phone: +44 (0) 20 8785 5995
Fax: +44 (0) 20 8785 5985
www.murdochbooks.co.uk
info@murdochbooks.co.uk

For Corporate Orders & Custom Publishing contact
Noel Hammond, National Business Development Manager, Murdoch Books Australia

Publisher: Sue Hines
Commissioning Editor: Anneka Manning
Design & illustrations: Hugh Ford
Photographer: Ian Wallace
Stylist: Louise Pickford
Editors: Belinda So and Katie Bosher
Food Editor: Christine Osmond
Home Economist: Grace Campbell
Project Editors: Laura Wilson and Claire Grady
Production Manager: Karen Small

Text © copyright Anna Gare 2013
Photography © Murdoch Books 2013
Illustrations © copyright Hugh Ford 2013

All rights reserved. No part of this publication may be reproduced, stored in a retrieval system or transmitted in any form or by any means, electronic, mechanical, photocopying, recording or otherwise, without the prior written permission of the publisher.

A cataloguing-in-publication entry is available from the catalogue of the National Library of Australia at www.nla.gov.au.

A catalogue record for this book is available from the British Library.

Colour reproduction by Splitting Image, Clayton, Victoria.

Printed by 1010 Printing International Limited, China.

IMPORTANT: Those who might be at risk from the effects of salmonella poisoning (the elderly, pregnant women, young children and those suffering from immune deficiency diseases) should consult their doctor with any concerns about eating raw eggs.

OVEN GUIDE: You may find cooking times vary depending on the oven you are using. We have used a fan-forced oven in these recipes. As a general rule, set the temperature for a conventional oven 20°C (35°F) higher than indicated in the recipe.

MEASURES GUIDE: We have used 20 ml (4 teaspoon) tablespoon measures. If you are using a 15 ml (3 teaspoon) tablespoon add an extra teaspoon of the ingredient for each tablespoon specified.